The Academy

ARTNEWS is published ten times a year, September-June;
and ARTNEWS ANNUAL [incorporating *Portfolio*],
each October, by Newsweek, Inc.
Address: 444 Madison Avenue, New York, N.Y. 10022
Telephone: TE 8-3730. Cables: Artenews, New York.

Subscription rates: Full subscription, consisting of ten
monthly issues of ARTNEWS and ARTNEWS ANNUAL,
$16.45 per year in U.S.A. Foreign postage,
$1.50 per year additional. Regular monthly issues of
ARTNEWS only, $11.50 per year in U.S.A.;
Foreign postage, $1.00 per year additional.
Single copies of ARTNEWS ANNUAL, $6.95 in U.S.A.
Foreign postage $.50 additional per copy.

ARTNEWS ANNUAL is distributed for
Newsweek, Inc. by The Macmillan Company,
866 Third Avenue, New York, N.Y. 10022.

European Advertising office for
Great Britain and Continental countries
Slade Fleming
ARTNEWS, 80 Haymarket, London, S.W. 1, England
Telephone: TRA 6166. Cables: Newsweek, London

Many artists, historians and critics have been of
invaluable help in preparing this volume. Particular
thanks, however, go to André Chastel in Paris, Milton Gendel
in Rome and Robert Rosenblum in New York.

Colorplate credits:

p. 12 Harry N. Abrams, New York
p. 13 Hermann, Paris
p. 14 Skira, Geneva
p. 18 Aldo Martello, Milan
p. 59 Prestel Verlag, Munich
p. 60 The Clarendon Press, Oxford; Pierre Tisné, Paris
p. 61 Phaidon Press, London
p. 62 American Horizon, New York
p. 65 Hermann, Paris

Art News Annual XXXIII

The Academy

Five Centuries of Grandeur and Misery,
from the Carracci to Mao Tse-tung

Edited by Thomas B. Hess and John Ashbery

Executive Editor	Harris Rosenstein
Senior Editor	Henry A. La Farge
Managing Editor	Elizabeth C. Baker
Associate Editor	Dolores Fenn
Design Director	Bradbury Thompson
Production Manager	Rena Shindelman
Production Assistant	Robert Preato
General Manager	Alvin Garfin
Publisher	Jack Fader
Advertising Manager	Roslyn E. Mandel
Advertising Assistant	Sephine B. Melrod

The Macmillan Company, New York

Johann Bernet: *Exact view of the arrangement of the paintings in the Salon of the Louvre, in 1785. Engraved from memory, and terminated during the time of the exhibition.*

Contents

The Academy

I

Some Academic Questions

By Thomas B. Hess

Academy, Academic, Academism (or Academicism)—these words mean "bad" in the conversations of the art community, much worse than "pretty" or "decorative" or even "sentimental"—they are about as dirty as polysyllables can get.

They do not refer to a category, like "Neo-Classic" or "Cubist," which are tags on rather specific, more or less homogeneous, bodies of material, but rather indicate areas where something unsettling has gone on, at any time, in any place. It is not unusual to hear some late Hellenistic sculpture called Academic or certain kinds of modern painting; witchdoctors it would seem can be just as Academic as Professors of Anatomical Draftsmanship.

When words become so heavily weighted, their pejorative charge can blur the qualities of the arts they denote. And when this happens, it becomes necessary to neutralize the slogan in order to examine what is beneath dispassionately (or even with an advocacy *for* rather than against; after all, it takes a positive pressure to overcome decades of negation, and in some of the essays that follow, the reader will find undisguised partisanship for the neglected Academicians under discussion).

It is one of the art historian's and critic's main responsibilities to present a work or a style free from distorting rhetoric and stereotypes—to let it appear as it is and as it was intended to be seen.

"Academic" means many things, but in art the label has been stuck especially hard on the later nineteenth-century painters, sculptors and architects who, in current popular mythology, played the Bad Guys against the Good Guys of Impressionism, Post-Impressionism, Expressionism and the other contemporaneous manifestations of the modern spirit. All artists in those days grew beards, but it is not as hard to distinguish between the artist sheep and goats as it is to identify the hirsute generals of opposing armies in 1860-1914. You can tell an Academician by the rosette in his buttonhole, his studied pose, frock coat; his fingernails are immaculate. The moderns, on the other hand, appear with bare buttonholes (Manet refused the Legion of Honor); their pants are baggy and they are given to sullen stares and to lounging on sofas. The Academicians, according to legend, are the ones who jeered at Manet and cheated him out of a triumph at the official Salons, whose juries and prizes they controlled. They raked in government commissions for mu-

rals and presidential portraits, captured the new-rich, often American, collectors, while Cézanne worked in lonely despair at Aix and van Gogh was, in Artaud's phrase, "suicided by society."

The nineteenth-century Academicians are popularly dismissed as eclectics, blind followers of the past, panderers to the most ludicrous demands of a parvenue middle-class; like stone walls they blocked the way to the future.

The myth has some truth to it as far as it goes which is not very deep. It ignores in its black or white interpretation all the nuances and interrelationships of the time. Art is not warfare; it has no losers; the "rubbish-heap of history" is stuffed with the masterpieces our grandchildren will admire. It is a fact that Academicians like Carolus-Duran and Gérome had more in common with Manet, from Manet's point of view, than he had with, for example, Gauguin. Almost all the great moderns were trained in the schools of the Academy (Gérome's pupils range from Eakins to Léger) and most of them accepted the fundamentals they had been taught. Cézanne's late *Bathers* makes little sense unless it is seen in its context of epic Salon painting; Degas' endless drawing from the model is in an Academic tradition which stretches from him through Ingres and Lebrun back to the Carracci; van Gogh was a fervent admirer of the illustrators of *Punch*. Proust, who had an eagle-eye for art and artists, based his Elstir more on Helleu than on Monet. One of Gauguin's last paintings in the South Seas is a version of a Puvis de Chavannes nymphet who could have walked out of a Napoleon III gilt frame. Matisse's odalisques relate to the Academic nude and Picasso's *Guernica* to the Academic "machine."

It is time, as Thérèse Burollet points out, to consider "Academic" as a descriptive adjective, like "Baroque" or "Classical," and not as a smear.

To discover what it means, we must begin with the accepted connotations and attempt to refine them.

Academic implies a worship of the past. But all artists have been in love with their ancestors: Matisse with Cézanne, Cézanne with Rubens, Rubens with Michelangelo, Michelangelo with the Master of the Belvedere Torso. Art comes out of art and artists have been hero-worshippers ever since the hero was invented. Indeed, it was the artist and the poet who invented the hero.

Academic art, however, does have a particular approach to the past; it tends to organize history in tidy straight lines.

Another indictment of the Academy is based upon its insistence on a doctrinaire, systematic esthetic. But this has characterized many other approaches too. Off-hand, one can cite Piero della Francesca, Alberti, Poussin and Mondrian as non-Academic artists who were involved in elaborating philosophical and technical systems, and one could add Seurat, Kandinsky and, in his own eccentric way, William Blake.

The Academy is built on doctrine, but of a special, metaphysical nature which, as will be seen, involves the concept of progress towards perfection.

Finally, the Academic is often confused with imitation, derivation and the arts of disciples. But almost every master, Academic or not, has had his following. Consider the crowds of minor Pointillists and Cubists, of the excellent and now largely forgotten school-artists around El Greco and Poussin. The issue of influence (and of misunderstood influence) applies to every kind of art.

At this point in our attempt at clarification, a brief chronology of the Academy is in order.

The word itself, of course, derives from the place near the Acropolis where Plato and his friends met to talk about philosophy. This was the original Grove of Academe and the men who walked under its trees were known as the Academy of Plato.

When the word was revived in Renaissance Florence by the Neo-Platonists in the circle of Pico della Mirandola and the Medici court, it was as a splendid banner proclaiming the modern humanist spirit of scientific inquiry and scholarship. The Florentine Academy was like Plato's—a group of colleagues coming together to discuss mutual interests. And not only were they advocates of the pursuit of the new knowledge, but they were also against the authoritarian labyrinths of scholasticism and the whole closed society of the Middle Ages. This strong anti-Guild, anti-craft, anti-medieval direction became the politics of the Academy for four centuries, sometimes moving it to establish dogmas whose rigidity and exaggerations can be understood only when the energetic opposition from the Guilds is taken into account.

The first artists' Academies (like the mysterious one referred to by Leonardo da Vinci in two of his prints) were, like the humanists', gatherings of peers for talk about matters of common interest. But the new Renaissance ideas in the arts were controversial and aggressively supported—which inevitably led those who championed them into teaching. Thus the schools which started in the sixteenth century and multiplied in the seventeenth in Italy, France and Central Europe named themselves "Academies" as a sign of the modernity of their approach and of their opposition to the Guilds' cumbersome regulations, apprenticeships and monopolistic practices (for example, the Guild Masters agitated for the old laws against the importation of foreign art and wanted to hold on to their franchises as the only artists and art merchants in town; ever since the days of William Morris, it has been a practice to sentimentalize the devoted craftsman and his honest day's labor, while forgetting that if he had had his way, Renaissance art would have been strangled at birth).

In the seventeenth and eighteenth centuries, as Nikolaus Pevsner points out in his excellent history of art academies, the new institutions developed in harmony with the growing centralization of European national states. The mercantilist sovereign who wanted to stimulate the manufacture of export items would patronize a local academy where modern teaching methods and a systematized esthetic would have a beneficial effect on techniques and standards of design. The art bureaucracy was a microcosm of the State's organization and expressed similar aims. The Academy could serve Mme. Pompadour's exquisite taste for the modern and, in the next century, the vitality, brutality and genius of industrial capitalism were perfectly furnished with forms and images decreed by the Academies of Fine Arts which flourished from St. Petersburg to Philadelphia.

The tendency of the Academy to become a school took an ironic turn in the 1920s when educationalists reincorporated Guild ideas and a new emphasis on crafts and industrial design into its system, most spectacularly in the Bauhaus. One of that school's illustrious directors, Mies van der Rohe, discoursed about the beauties of a simple brick with an eloquence which could only have been matched by that of a Romanesque master-mason explaining the cathedral of Chartres.

But until the ultimate irony of the Bauhaus, the Academy had, and where it continues to exist, still has, a corpus of ideas about art and the role of the artist which in themselves define the Academic point of view—that is, if we are willing to keep pejorative implications in suspension.

First of all, the Academy inherited from its Neo-Platonic ancestry a dedication to the belief that art is an intellectual discipline. The High Renaissance Academicians initiated a curriculum which teaches concepts first and methods afterwards (techniques were considered so simple that anyone could master them with a little practice). They started their students with the most abstract ideas, i.e. perspective and proportion (of the figure) and only later were pupils allowed to move on to drawing and painting or carving.

Being intellectual, art should be systematic, the Academicians reasoned; it should be divisible into logical categories and a hierarchy of modes. An order of rank was established with History Painting at the top and still-life at the bottom of the ladder. And each aspect of art was studied, separated into its components, analyzed. Artists were taught to draw the parts of the body before they approached the whole figure. They studied the hand, the foot, the mouth, the anatomy of the horse bone by bone and muscle by muscle. (An almost identical conclusion was reached by the great Chinese Orthodox masters when they set out to formulate an esthetic. The Oriental text on how to paint a picture, called the *Mustard Seed Garden Painter's Manual*, could have been written by the director of the French Academy in Rome and read with approval by Sir Joshua Reynolds.)

As knowledge increases, it follows that art should progress; for example, anatomy becomes more precise and thus better; perspective renders more difficult vistas with greater exactitude; archaisms are weeded out of historical tableaux.

Informing this rational structure was the conviction that art is a profession as important as any other specialized calling, whether medicine, jurisprudence or mathematics. The artist was no longer a medieval journeyman filling orders for public or private patrons, but a liberated man in pursuit of the Truth as he sees it.

Progress and Truth are abstract ideas and the forms in Academic art became abstract forms. The student did not study any noses or toes, but the perfect nose and toe. As in science, the specific is only a step on the way to the general. Thus the Academy stood (and stands) for High Art which, in turn, strives for Ideal Beauty, at first envisioned as a dream of Greece shaped by Rome and Raphael, and more recently as an ultimate, absolute abstraction or a field of pure color.

Given these assumptions, history will be seen as a straight line.

Assume Ideal Beauty is point A, placed on the right side of a sheet of paper.

Imagine point B, the painting under consideration, a few inches to its left.

Scatter to the left of point B about a million dots, representing all the other paintings in the world.

Now sight back from A to B and then project the line into the random crowd of artists of the past.

Erase all the dots that do not lie on the sight-line.

Result: a clear simple straight history of art. Raphael begat Annibale Carracci who begat Poussin who begat Lebrun who had many children and grandchildren including Vien, who was the teacher of J. L. David, who begat Ingres, etc. Or to take a more recent formulation: Monet to Matisse to Miro to Pollock to Morris Louis, etc.

This, it must be emphasized, is Academic doctrine as preached by Academic critics. History rests more lightly on the backs of artists who, looking inward rather than backward, take a more catholic, jaunty view of the past.

The Academicians formed and fought for their ideology with tenacious seriousness. There is the famous anecdote about Ingres hooding his face in a cloak when forced to walk through a gallery in which paintings by Delacroix were hanging. And about Gérome barring the path of Loubet, President of the Republic, to the rooms where some Impressionists were exhibited, with the phrase: "Stop, Mister President; here lies the disgrace of France!"

Once we comprehend what they stand for, we can try to draw up a balance-sheet between the Academics and the non- (or anti-) Academics. It does not tell so badly against the former as the Good Guys vs. Bad Guys confrontation has led so many contemporary critics to assume.

For the Academy:

It keeps in mind the level of High Art, of ambitious projects that will rival the masterpieces of the past while advancing towards the Ideal.

It insists on the intellectual content of art, even though its basic assumptions may be such mystical convictions as the Perfection of Greece, Inspiration, the Condition of Music, the Probity of Line, Pure Color. All rationales are founded on such murk, but the Academy exfoliates its ideas with rigorous logic, and in the process performs a valuable service in the fight against cant. Art, after all, *is* a matter of brains. Furthermore, the Academy has been one of the most sensitive recorders of its own times. It has preserved the moods, hopes, anxieties, the erotic fantasies and patriotic fevers of the milieu. A study of the *Zeitgeist* of Paris during one of the great moments in the history of Western culture can be profitably undertaken in an examination of the now neglected *pompiers:* the Salon heroes who have been so glibly dismissed by a later generation of critics devoted to Utrillo or Chagall. If the image of Mallarmé is found in Manet, Baudelaire preferred Rops; and parallels to Balzac, Maupassant, Barbey d'Aurevilly or Zola may be sought in Gervex, Bonnat, Raffaëlli, Béraud and Steinlen as well as among the famous Impressionists.

The alienation of the artist from society, a more dubious accomplishment, is also partly due to the Academy. In its wars against the feudal Guilds, it first declared the artist independent of the patron, then free from class barriers, finally an equal to the gods. In winning this liberty for self-expression, the Academy also bequeathed to thousands of artists the right to starve in bitterness and isolation. It probably would have happened anyway, without the interventions of the humanists and classicists. The cultural gap is an inevitable part of the modern landscape. But the fact remains that it was the Academy which cut the vital tissues that kept the medieval artists securely bound to the social organism.

Against the Academy:

Its dependence on doctrine led it to exclude and hamper many artists whose natures were more open, at once more self-doubting and more self-reliant. People who know that they hold the Truth, who are convinced of the existence of absolutes, of historical necessity, of what is right and who is wrong, are usually bigots. The Academicians had (and have) the vice in abundance.

When, in this century, dictators in Russia, Italy and Germany liquidated the avant-garde, it was as much through the promptings of reactionary Beaux-Arts professors as it was from any political decision. A glance at the record of commissions for major sculptural projects given by the U.S. government in the past decades reveals how firmly the Academic artists can hold to their sinecures.

Art can be said to exist in a dialectical tension between the messy and the neat. The Academy breaks the tension and tries to eliminate all mess. Its cult of Ideal Beauty, its incessant war against what Hegel called "alien nature," can be seen as a will to order, but also as a flight from chaos—from the delirium of Mannerism in the seventeenth century, from the extravagances of the Rococo in the eighteenth, from the banalities of Realism in the nineteenth, from the dark emotional side of Abstract-Expressionism in the twentieth. And in cleaving so fast to one end of the antithesis, the flight from chaos has led many into a desert of neatness.

But this is a trap for artists who follow critics too closely and for critics who run too fast after their own reputations. Many Academic painters found an inner balance and a place for themselves within a great tradition. Modern art could never have evolved in all its wonderful richness and profundity without the interventions of these austere masters who were proud of their public success, their redoubtable talents and most of all the title, *Academician.*

Jean-Louis-Ernest Meissonier: *The Palace of the Tuileries after the Commune,* 1871 (Compiègne museum). The view through the ruined windows of the palace, one of the major architectural casualties of the Commune, is toward the Triumphal Arch of the Carrousel, whose bronze chariot group by Bosio, 1828, symbolizes the Restoration of the Bourbon monarchy. The Latin text at the bottom reads: "The glory of the ancients remains beyond the flames— May, 1871." See essay by Salvador Dali beginning on page 108.

Nicolas Poussin

Poussin: *The Nurture of Jupiter*, ca. 1640
(38 inches high). State Museums, Berlin-Dahlem.
See essay by Jacques Thuillier beginning on page 28.

Charles Le Brun: The Galerie d'Hercule, detail of the
ceiling fresco, about 1650-51. Hotel Lambert, Paris.
See essay by Jacques Thuillier beginning on page 28.

Simon Vouet: *The Virgin with a Twig*, 1640 (32½ inches high).
Collection of Walter P. Chrysler, Jr., New York.

Reynolds: *Cupid as a Link Boy,* ca. 1777
(30 inches high). Albright-Knox Art Gallery,
Buffalo, N.Y. See page 44.

Sir Joshua Reynolds: *Lady Caroline Howard,* ca. 1778
(56¼ inches high). National Gallery, Washington, D.C.
See essay by John Russell beginning on page 38.

Lady Caroline Howard
Lady Cawdor

Above: Annibale Carracci's *Apollo and Marsyas*, ca. 1597-1604, detail of ceiling, Farnese Palace, Rome.
Below: Detail of Annibale Carracci's *Flight into Egypt*, ca. 1604. Doria Gallery, Rome.

II

The Carracci: A Family Academy

By Milton J. Lewine

An authority on the sixteenth- and seventeenth-century art and
architecture of Rome, where he spends each summer, Milton J. Lewine
is associate professor of art history at Columbia. He is co-editor
of two recent volumes of essays presented to Rudolph Wittkower.

Every Sunday morning in Rome a large crowd slowly gathers
before the Palazzo Farnese, waiting for 11 A.M. when the
palace, now the French embassy, is opened to the public—
except in August—for just one hour. Of course the visitors
are drawn by the architecture of Sangallo the Younger
and Michelangelo, but the courtyard can be seen any time.
The Sunday attraction is once again, after some 150 years of
popular neglect, Annibale Carracci's fresco decorations of
the Gallery (1597-1604). Noble and festive, sumptuous and
melodic, Annibale's frescoes established a new style in Rome,
a vigorous style of solid and sculpturesque forms moving
easily in an atmospheric space of color and light—in sum, the
Early Baroque.

Annibale and his great contemporary Caravaggio together
altered the course of Western painting, but historically Annibale's work reached wider in its consequences. Caravaggio
was a fierce independent who worked without assistants,
only in oils, and directly onto the canvas with little or no
preparation. At first in Rome he painted genre and mythological subjects, but he reached his full maturity in religious
pictures, such as the famous *Calling of Matthew,* works that
offered a seeming realism, a shocking and fresh interpretation of subject, and a hard strong lighting that falls through
an eerie space of deep, mysterious shadow. Generations of
artists learned from Caravaggio, but they had to learn sub-
jectively, on the whole working alone, absorbing what they
wanted experimentally, but rarely penetrating deep into
his idiosyncratic style.

Annibale's case is just the reverse. His powerful style is
composed of rational forms, often rooted in tradition and
always carefully achieved through various stages of pre-
paratory drawing. He worked in oils throughout his life,
but he preferred the time-honored medium of fresco, used
in monumental decorations like the Farnese Gallery, the
kind and class of painting that stood above all others in
Renaissance and Baroque thinking. The very clarity of
Annibale's forms made them accessible through the medium
of drawing, and his working methods offered young artists
everywhere an objective means of learning and producing
works of their own, with assistants or without.

The origins of Annibale's Roman style and method lie
in Bologna, formed in the milieu of the Carracci Academy.
This Academy, so influential in other ways as well, is the
subject of our investigation, but the job is not easy. The
sources are incomplete, the evidence is often only indirect,
and many points are still debatable. Nevertheless we can
piece together at least a fair account of the Academy and
its goals.

Around 1580 Bolognese art was dominated by a Late-Man-
nerist style, as represented by the work of the brilliant Pellegrino Tibaldi or the typical Orazio Samacchini. Characteristic are the highly sophisticated and complex designs, artificial poses, exaggerated but weightless bodies, unnatural colors and an airless, illogical space. The three Carracci—Annibale (b. 1560), his brother Agostino (b. 1557) and their
cousin Ludovico (b. 1555)—were naturally trained in this
style, but under the leadership of Ludovico in the early
1580s they began to rebel. Tired of an art ruled by Florentine and Roman Mannerism, they turned to new models to
help them shape their still instinctive new ideas: to Correg-

Mannerist precursors in Bologna: Pellegrino Tibaldi's
Ulysses Blinding Polyphemus, fresco, ca. 1555 (Palazzo
dell' Università, Bologna); and [below] Orazio Samacchini's
Coronation of the Virgin, ca. 1575 (Pinacoteca, Bologna).

The Carracci: A Family Academy

gio at Parma, to the great Venetians and to a direct confrontation with nature itself. And to help them in their search they founded an academy in Bologna, the *Accademia degli Incamminati*, probably in 1582 when Ludovico was 27 years old, Agostino 25 and Annibale all of 22. Thus the Academy began as a youthful affair, rebellious, engaged in something new and assertively optimistic—the *Incamminati* were "those who had set out on the road," obviously to a new and better style. The Academy was successful right from the start, attracting young and progressive artists from many other workshops besides the Carracci's own. This wide appeal points up a distinction that must be kept in mind, for the workshop (*bottega*) was a private concern organized to produce works of art while the Academy was separate in function and place, a kind of club under Carracci direction, but open to all who would share in its artistic aims and financial expense.

The program focused on the traditional and central element of Italian art and theory, the human body. For study purposes the Carracci assembled plaster casts of whole figures, of torsos and of parts of the body. The Carracci were all devoted to study in detail. Ludovico had a favorite cast of hands and Agostino took the model of an ear with him on

Drawing from the model at the Bolognese Academy: [below left] Annibale Carracci's *Seated Youth* (Uffizi, Florence); and his cousin Ludovico's *Figure Study*, ca. 1585, black crayon heightened with white chalk (Windsor Castle).

The Carracci systematically studied the figure in each of its parts: Agostino's
Feet drawn over an earlier sketch for an Annunciation, ca. 1595. Windsor Castle.

III

The Birth of the Beaux-Arts

By Jacques Thuillier

Professor of art history at the University of Dijon and an expert
on Poussin and his school, Jacques Thuillier is at work on a major
book on the roots of art criticism in the seventeenth century.

Discussions of the Academy of Painting and Sculpture during the *"Grand Siècle"* usually refer to it as a political instrument in the service of the monarchy. Louis XIV had subordinated to his throne the country's nobility, until then the most fractious in Europe; the Church, always jealous of its rights; the Parliamentarians, who not long before had nearly done away with the throne; and the writers, henceforth unanimous—thanks to the "French Academy"—in their praise of the "Sun King." It remained to discipline the artists, to impose uniform principles on them, to employ them for the glory of the State—and first of all the King; hence that admirable invention, the Royal Academy.

But this convenient, conventional image is completely false.

Perhaps Colbert had such intentions when, as minister, he began to reorganize the Academy from 1663 on, but it was founded in 1648. Louis XIV was then 10 years old. The Parliament controlled Paris; the Regent and the little king were to be forced to flee the city by night for safety's sake; the French came very near to abolishing monarchy, as the English actually did a few months later. How, in these conditions, could the Academy have been an offshoot of royal Absolutism?

On the other hand, a closer examination shows that the members of the new organization were not greybeards anxious to dominate the arts: only 10 or 12, at most, were over 40. The majority were between 30 and 35 and Le Brun, who led them almost from the start, was only 29. They comprised in Paris what today would be called "the young painters." Their Academy, at the outset, was very much like an avant-garde movement.

One must remember that an Academy, in the seventeenth century, was primarily one of many institutions where young men of good families went after college to perfect themselves: to learn riding, fencing and all such "noble and honest" arts: in short, to acquire finish. This contemporary sense of the word connoted at once youth, nobility and elegance. It was also applied, in the Italian sense, to private meetings at which people of good taste indulged a shared passion: music, natural sciences, philosophy or poetry. Such groups quickly multiplied (Miss Frances Yates some time ago published a brilliant account of them). Many important people had their own little academy, and it was natural for Richelieu, whose pet failing was literature, to have thought of starting his own: thus the "French Academy" began. It brought together, not the greatest writers, but men of letters and men of the world interested in poetry or the novel, and they were quite young: Conrart was 31, Habert de Montmort and Faret 34 and the abbé de Cerisy 20. The only difference was that Richelieu wanted his Academy to outshine all others and, as head of State, made it an official institution, with various privileges for its members. The most valued of these was perhaps the "right of commitimus" by which all legal affairs could be withdrawn from the common courts: a precious favor in a time when the most obliging

Louis XIV's great minister Colbert, at the urging of Le Brun, gave the French Academy its definitive form, in 1663, modeled after his ideal of the centralized state. This portrait of Colbert was inserted by Le Brun into a *Resurrection of Christ*. Lyon museum.

man had at least three or four lawsuits on his hands. It greatly strengthened the institution.

Did Richelieu and his right arm, Sublet de Noyers, the Superintendent of Buildings, think not long after about founding an Academy of Painting? Possibly. Certain texts, rather obscure yet not to be wholly discounted, imply that an initial Company was founded under their aegis. They may have wished to profit from Poussin's taking up residence in Paris at the end of 1640. But it was not that easy a task. It was necessary to find accomplished, genteel artists to talk to the great seigneurs and collectors about their art, and there were not many of them then. Besides Poussin there was Stella, a cultured man who had just received the coveted title of Chevalier of St. Michael; "Monsieur" Champaigne, whom Marie de' Medicis and Richelieu admired for his lofty spirit and incorruptible life no less than for his painting; Simon Vouet, who was known as a gentleman; La Hyre, passionately interested in hunting, music and

mathematics: these painters were what was needed, but how to get them together? Vouet wanted to be first in everything; he was jealous of the Cardinal's esteem for Champaigne, and the arrival of Poussin, who was immediately swamped with favors and commissions, had decisively split Parisian painters into two opposed cliques, each with its backers and protectors. It would have taken all the Cardinal's personal influence to form a viable Academy in this situation. And he died at the end of 1642, followed shortly by King Louis XIII. He certainly hadn't had time to give this fledgling Academy the status of an official institution; yet the idea had been born.

It was soon developed under the pressure of events. One must remember here the paradoxical situation of Paris painters in the seventeenth century. Considered mere trades, painting and sculpture were part of the medieval guild system, and their regulations went back to 1391. The "Community," as it was called, had the exclusive right to practice

Sébastien Bourdon's portrait of Martin de Charmois, first patron of the Academy, aristocrat, secret painter. Beaux-Arts, Paris.

Le Brun's portrait of his friend the painter Louis Testelin, ca. 1650, one of the mainstays of the young Academy. Louvre.

Self-portrait of Le Brun, 1684, at the height of his power; but it must not be forgotten that behind this old master covered with honors is the spirit of an ambitious, brilliantly gifted young man. Uffizi, Florence.

The dashing young Le Brun at the time he founded the Academy, possibly a self-portrait, holding a picture. Versailles museum.

the arts in Paris. Under penalty of imprisonment or fine, no one could handle a brush, or even sell a painting, unless he had obtained the title of "master," or had worked in the studio and under the control of a "master." And it was not easy to get a mastership: if one wasn't the son of a "master," one had to undergo a long phase as apprentice and guild-brother, or buy it at a high price—unless one preferred to marry a "master's" widow—dim outlook for the young painters arriving from the provinces with the desire to make a name in the capital, or for those who had gone to Rome to study the works of the great painters. The majority tried to find some loop-hole. The best way was to get a "King's Commission": such *"commissionaires"* were automatically freed from corporative regulations. But patronage was needed for this—or money. The commonest way was to live in some "privileged place" such as those within the jurisdiction of big monasteries, or a college in the Latin Quarter. Many young painters newly arrived from their native regions did this, including Poussin and Champaigne, who at the beginning of their careers lived for a time in the College of Laon, or Lubin Baugin and the three Le Nain brothers, who lived outside the city in a neighborhood attached to the monastery of St. Germain-des-Prés.

It irritated the Guild of master painters to see the best young men escape its authority in this way, especially because most of its own members were, except for a few recognized talents, mere daubers; many knew only how to gild,

or paint coach-doors, store-signs and St. Nicholases for country priests. These mediocrities were forced to recognize that the big commissions were going elsewhere and that their work was not valued as highly. There was not much they could do about the "privileged places," protected by ancient traditions. They chose instead to attack the *"commissionaires."* The Regency period offered a sudden opportunity for paying off old grudges. Backed by the bourgeoisie and the people of Paris, Parliament was in open conflict with the monarchy, a sufficient pretext for magistrates to declare illegal the freedom of the "King's painters" or the "Queen's painters," if only to curtail royal power. The "jurymen masters" then staged their attack: in 1647 they got what amounted to a decree from Parliament giving them satisfaction by virtually putting the *"commissionaires"* at their mercy. But the result was not as they had planned: without knowing it, they had motivated the Academy's formation.

The proscribed painters were not content to answer by legal means; they realized the danger. A small group met fairly often at the house of Juste d'Egmont, a fashionable portraitist, under the patronage of M. de Charmois. The latter was a rather important person, who had a strong love for painting and even painted in secret; at his death a number of his own works were discovered in his house; unluckily they are all lost, and we shall never know if he was a clumsy amateur or an unknown genius. He was the consistent defender of the *"commissionaires."* He demonstrated to the Regent and Mazarin without much difficulty that the machinations of the Guild were a personal insult. The idea of an Academy was brought up again. Besides Juste d'Egmont, there was Sarrazin the sculptor and Corneille the painter; other artists had joined them, notably the young Le Brun, who had returned from Rome two years before. He had important protection (in particular that of Chancellor Séguier), a taste for intrigue and a talent for organization that was capable both of formulating principles and of effective action. He was not long in becoming the leader. Things went well, and the Royal Academy of Painting and Sculpture was officially instituted on January 20, 1648, at a Regency counsel, and its letters of patent were confirmed on March 9. Already meetings had been held; several painters joined the "founders," in particular the widely respected Philippe de Champaigne and the three Le Nain brothers. It was decided to have "public exercises," to conduct a school in which future painters, freed from the traditions of the workshop, would get a modern education based on a study of the live model. Resistance was organized against the attacks of the furious Guild. By an invisible process, the "society of choice spirits" became a "syndicate of professional defense."

It would be too long and tedious to list all the difficulties of the young Academy. Born of necessity, created in enthusiasm, it was soon to encounter the worst obstacles: envy and poverty. It had taken care to remain young: it admitted Champaigne, but did not seek the patronage of Poussin, who had returned to Rome, but who could have helped the new institution with his ever-increasing moral authority.

Jacques Stella was forgotten and the ambitious Simon Vouet carefully ignored. The latter, in revenge, took charge of the Guild, reformed its leadership and instituted a curriculum copied from the Academy. No doubt he would have prevailed if he had not died prematurely in the following year, 1649. The rivalry continued. Enthusiasm slowly ebbed, and voluntary contributions came in less often. An alliance with the Guild was negotiated; it failed soon after. Le Brun sustained the members' courage, but was himself replaced by the ambitious Charles Errard, a very good painter, today totally forgotten, but who in his lifetime was considered at least the equal of Le Brun or Le Sueur, and who enjoyed powerful protection.

Nevertheless, circumstances again favored them. The bickerings of the Fronde alienated the public; the royal power invoked by the Academy regained its authority. The Superintendent of Buildings threw all his support behind the new institution, and by 1654 managed to get for its members the famous privilege of "commitimus" given to the members of the French Academy. When Mazarin died, and the young Louis XIV decided to take the government into his own hands, assigning Colbert to reorganize the State, it became evident that the Academy's future was assured. Protected by both Séguier and Colbert, Le Brun was returned to his position, more powerful than ever. He was behind Colbert's reform by which the Company's privileges were consolidated and its status clearly defined. Placed under the royal patronage, its members henceforth definitively escaped the control of the old guilds. The right to conduct a school was reserved to the Academy, and it was Colbert's idea to resume regular public lectures. In 1666, the founding of the French Academy in Rome, where the best students were to finish their training in contact with the Italian masterpieces, completed the process. The idea of painting as a Liberal Art had won a total victory: a new phase began for the Academy, this time as one of the State's principal cultural institutions.

Is this to say that the young painters of 1648 had "arrived," and were now anxious themselves to dominate the

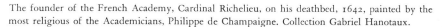

The founder of the French Academy, Cardinal Richelieu, on his deathbed, 1642, painted by the most religious of the Academicians, Philippe de Champaigne. Collection Gabriel Hanotaux.

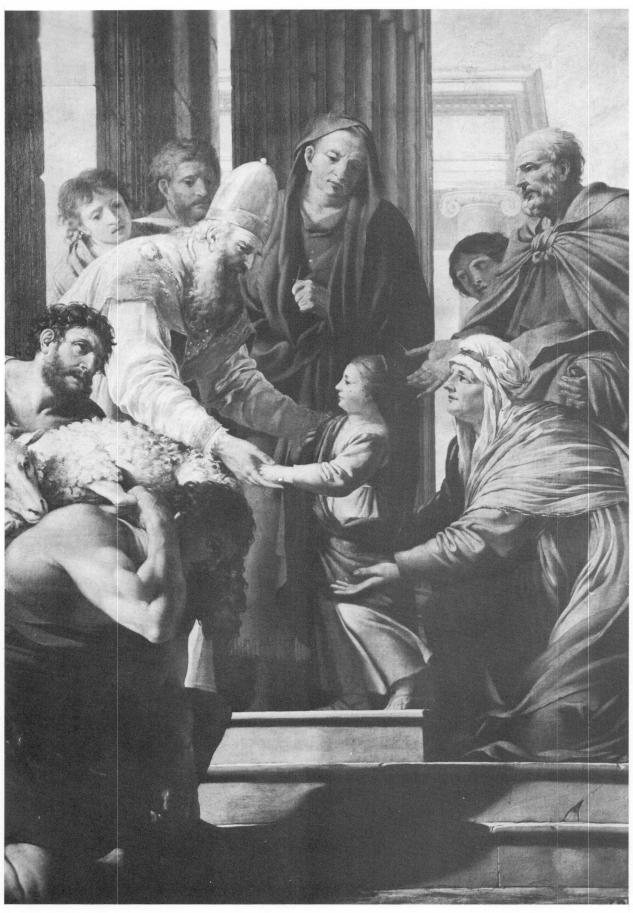

The Presentation in the Temple, newly attributed to the little-known seventeenth-century master Michel Corneille. Dijon museum.

The Academy always had its liberal side. This genre scene was the diploma picture of Mme. Therbouche, an elderly, ugly, Prussian lady who was nonetheless welcomed by the membership in 1767.

As the illustrations on this page indicate, the Academy had no precise esthetic doctrine at its beginnings. Corneille, Bourdon and Vignon all played important roles in its formation, but all took different stylistic approaches. *The Continence of Scipio* [above] by Sébastien Bourdon. Museum of Fine Arts, Grenoble.

By Simon Vouet, great enemy of the Academy who set up a rival organization: *Allegory of Wealth*. Louvre.

St. Paul the Hermit and St. Anthony by Vignon. Epinal museum.

arts, establish rules and leave to their successors an instrument for dictatorship of taste and intellectual sclerosis? In the past certain writers, thinking of the Academy of their own day, have believed so. Again, nothing could be more false. Here as elsewhere Le Brun and Colbert had created the institution required by the time, which would remain useful and necessary up to the French Revolution.

As a matter of fact, from the 1660s until 1793, nothing of importance was to happen in Paris painting that was not directly connected with the Academy. All the great or near-great painters were members: for example Watteau, who painted his famous *Embarkation for Cythera* as his diploma-piece, or Boucher or Chardin, one of the Company's most

influential and devoted members. Fragonard resigned from it, yet owed it everything he was; it would not be an exaggeration to say that he had long been its pet. J.-L. David destroyed it at the time of the Revolution, but as an ungrateful son: it had done much for his success.

Is it necessary to go on? If French art at the end of the seventeenth century and during the eighteenth century kept its vitality, avoiding the sclerosis that obtained in the great Italian centers (except for Venice, Rome and Naples), and those of Spain and the Netherlands, it was mainly because of the Academy.

From its beginning, it had kept the custom of admitting young artists. Membership was not a reward for a long ca-

Clytie by Charles de La Fosse: one of the more delicate, lyrical painters of the Academy, he was stimulated by its hot debates on the importance of color. Versailles museum.

The meaning of this curious picture, and of its sketch in Stockholm, remains obscure, but its anonymous 17th-century author obviously portrayed a studio joke which refers directly to the French Academy and its awards. Private collection, Florence.

reer and gold medals in the Salon, as was the future Institute of France that succeeded it in the nineteenth century: painters were often accepted before they were 30 years old. It also preserved a sense of liberty; the "Company" remained open-minded. It was one of the few institutions of the old régime that admitted women—a practice begun by Le Brun himself in 1663. Simple amateurs, critics and well-known collectors were received as "honorary members." Discussions were unrestricted, sometimes quite passionate. The quarrels over color that broke out in 1671 and eventually transformed French painting, the reaction against "modern chicory" (or Rococo) and the return to the classics, found in the Academy a propitious base and propaganda outlet. The Company's members began to show in a "Salon" in the seventeenth century; these exhibitions became more and more regular and turned into one of the set features of Paris life. Its importance can hardly be exaggerated. There had never been such

direct contact before with the public, which until then had had to content itself with the latest commissioned altarpieces, with the painting offered to Notre Dame each year in May, or with the small paintings on sale at painters' studios or dealers' shops. This vast assemblage of contrasted portraits, still-lifes, genre paintings or immense historical "machines" presented all the latest works at once, brought all new developments to light and forced the painter to be of his time. Far from imposing uniform rules, the Academy encouraged debates, allowed comparisons to be made and incited innovation. Far from being a restraint, it hastened the evolution of art—not to say its revolutions. And, by a sort of paradox, it was to be the same Academy, reformed by the Revolution, that gradually forgot this function, and became the watchdog of moribund traditions.

Translated from the French by Lane Dunlop.

Reynolds' Rembrandtesque self-portrait as a prestigious academician, a bust of Michelangelo at his side: he wears the robes of a recent honorary doctorate from Oxford, 1773, a year he was also complimented with the mayoralty of Plympton, his home town. Royal Academy.

IV

Sir Joshua, P.R.A.

By John Russell

John Russell is art critic of the London *Sunday Times,* and author
of books on Seurat, Braque and Delacroix. He has made a special
study of Reynolds and his relation to eighteenth-century painting.

Sir Joshua Reynolds is not loved. He is respected, he is
"placed" in accordance with the rules of *le fairplay,* and in
a quiet way he is admired. But loved? That is quite a different thing. The man is rare who would put his hand in
the fire for the first President of our Royal Academy, the
close friend of Johnson and Goldsmith and Garrick and
Burke, the painter of *Sarah Siddons as The Tragic Muse* or
the author of the *Discourses.* William Blake's opinion—
"This Man Was Hired to Depress Art"—has gained a great
deal of ground, and Goldsmith's estimate of Reynolds' manners—"gentle, complying and bland"—has come to stand
for his work also.

Above all, we prize the quality that Reynolds never had
and never claimed to have: the recklessness of individual
genius. People would rather write on individualists of the
second rank like Zoffany or Marcellus Laroon than on Reynolds, foremost among the English generalizers. Once again
it is Blake who sets the tone: "The following Discourse," he
wrote in his copy of Reynolds' *Works,* "is particularly Interesting to Blockheads as it endeavours to prove that There
is No such thing as Inspiration & that any Man of a plain
Understanding may by Thieving from Others become a
Mich Angelo." For generations, Reynolds was shunned by
painters and critics alike as if some kind of contamination
were inherent in his stately and magnanimous periods. Ruskin annotated his copy of the *Discourses* in a manner hardly
less injurious than Blake's, and it was left to Roger Fry in
1905 to make a counter-estimate of our first P.R.A.

"It is just because Reynolds had the gift, an unusual one
among artists, of rising to a general view of art as a whole,

and of regarding his own performance with objective impar-
tiality, that he is so remarkable as a critic": this was the first
of Fry's points, and his main reason for re-editing the *Discourses.* The second point made by Fry was that Reynolds'
procedures were marked by a personal generosity that was
rare at the time and has not become more common since.
He was, in fact, "intensely optimistic about the future of
art in England, and looked forward to a generation which
should surpass himself as much as, or more than, he had
surpassed Hudson and Richardson." Better art in a more
comprehending world: that was what Reynolds was after.

But the better art, when it came, was not of the sort
that he had had in mind, and the more comprehending
world swerved away from the *Discourses* and regarded
them as, at best, an interesting monument to a minor artist.
It is among art historians, and not among artists, that Reynolds has lately had something of a revival. Ever since 1930,
when Edgar Wind pioneered the subject, scholars have enjoyed tracing the sources of Reynolds' vocabulary, and his
taste for the Bolognese masters has come back into fashion
in a way which would have astonished even Roger Fry.
Reynolds the theorist now stands higher than at any time
since his death, and E. K. Waterhouse carried his colleagues
with him when he wrote in the 1940s that the *Discourses*
are "the most practical, the most sensible and the best-
written discussion of the theory of painting in the English
language."

"Practical" and "sensible" are deflationary adjectives, even
so, and most readers still prefer the clouded and fragmen-
tary insights of individual genius. Reynolds' *Discourses*

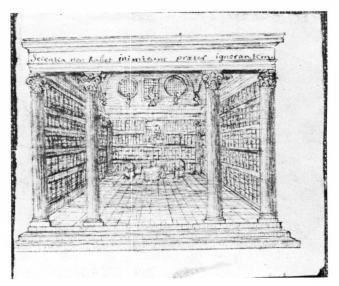

At age 8, Reynolds drew this library, inscribed "Wisdom has no enemy save ignorance." Royal Academy, London.

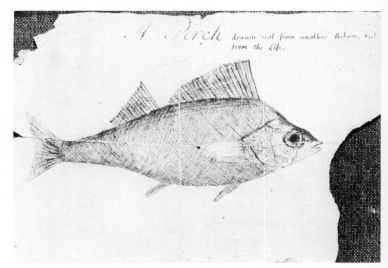

Schoolboy drawing Reynolds proudly inscribed, "A Perch, drawn not from another Picture, but from the Life." Royal Academy, London.

1757 sketch of one of Reynolds' regular card-playing companions, the radical John Wilkes. Royal Academy.

Sir Joshua, P.R.A.

could be subtitled "How to Paint Good Pictures if You Start with My Disadvantages." Their manner is august, formal and level-headed: we have only to look at Gainsborough's letters or at Constable's to make contact with wayward, arrowy, plain-spoken, irresistible natures. We like a painter to be his own man, absolutely, and we rather despise

anyone who abrogates his own personality in favor of a general idea. But Reynolds saw the art of the future as a systematic and a synthetic art, in which painters would pick over the past and make use of such elements within it as complied with "the great universal truth of things." "The daily food and nourishment of the mind of an Artist is to be found," he wrote, "in the great works of his predecessors. There is no other way for him to become great himself."

All this looks to us today like a straight misreading of the English genius. Nothing is farther from the natural instincts of that genius than the kind of sedulous patchwork which Reynolds had in mind. The inspired borrowings, to our way of thinking, are those we don't notice: Gainsborough's use of Rubens, for instance. And although we find it comical that Constable should have almost dreaded the foundation of the National Gallery, on the ground that it would mean the end of the British School, we also know what Constable meant. Constable distinguished between the Old Masters as a guide to correct behavior and the Old Masters as a dead weight: Reynolds ranked correct behavior above all things.

He also had in mind a hierarchy of ambitions which subsequent generations have not upheld. In a canceled passage quoted by Prof. Hilles he wrote that "The exertion of the mental faculties gives the superiority to the Painter of History over all others of our profession." This was not in point of fact either a foolish or an unfeeling remark, and it reflected an opinion then generally acted upon: between 1769 and 1801, for instance, Benjamin West was paid more than a million dollars in today's money for history-paintings delivered to the Crown. There is still much to be said for the huge decorations on the subject of "The Progress of Human Culture" which James Barry painted between 1777 and 1783 for the Society of Arts. J. S. Copley's *Brook Watson and the Shark* of 1778, now in Boston, looks forward to Géricault. When Boydell handed out commissions for his

Shakespeare Gallery, from 1789 onwards, there was a real chance that minor masterpieces would result.

The ironical thing is that history and the history-painters were pulling in different directions. History was moving towards an art of immediate sensation: Reynolds favored majestic, long-pondered procedures in which spontaneity played almost no part. His ideal student would have put Equilibrium before all things: but the man who really believed in history-painting was Haydon, and Haydon went out of his mind. Above all, Reynolds himself was hopelessly bad at history-painting. Few things are more painful for the champion of British art than the small back room in the Hermitage where hang the two large paintings commissioned from Reynolds by Catherine the Great. The *Infant Hercules* and the *Continence of Scipio* dispose once and for all of the idea that in the case of Reynolds precept and practice were one. The only "great universal truth" which emerges from these monuments of ineptitude is the fact that people should know their own limitations.

Reynolds' genius, in so far as he had it at all, lay in what he regarded as a second-rate department of art. His theorizing can, in fact, be regarded as a vast compensatory operation, just as his dependence upon society can be interpreted as a by-product of fear and anxiety. Dr. Johnson was perhaps the closest of his friends and the author of the sonorous Dedication which prefaces the *Discourses*, but even Dr. Johnson allowed himself a disparaging remark to the effect that Reynolds was "zealous for nothing"; and Northcote, for years his close associate, accused him of "a want of that firm and manly courage and honor which is so absolutely necessary to the highest degree of rectitude." Northcote was not on oath, of course, and he was not a man to be believed absolutely; but it may well be true that Reynolds' unvarying blandness in public life got him into scrapes. He was too good a judge of painting not to realize that when a Northcote or an Angelica Kauffmann undertook to adapt the Italian masters, the result more often than not was simply ludicrous. Northcote cannot have been

the only painter who felt himself let down when Reynolds weighed the result against the intention and felt the scales come down with a thump on the wrong side.

He could have said, if taxed with these incidents, that his Discourse of 1782 made it perfectly clear that he never authorized mere imitation of the Old Masters. "The great business of study," he said quite clearly, "is to form a *mind*, adapted and adequate to all times and all occasions": in the case of a Northcote or a Kauffmann that mind was negligible. In Reynolds' own case, the mind was equal to all emergencies and it functioned as well in relation to society as to art. Reynolds was not one to go against society

Reynolds' *Boswell*, 1786 (28½ inches high), a friend portrayed formally. National Portrait Gallery, London.

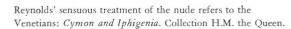

Reynolds' sensuous treatment of the nude refers to the Venetians: *Cymon and Iphigenia*. Collection H.M. the Queen.

A late example of Reynolds' high classical doctrine: *The Death of Dido*, 1781. Buckingham Palace.

(though he did stand out against the King of England, to the point of being physically unable to compose a dedication to him, and he never seems to have learned that the spelling "Prince of Whales" was unlikely to be accepted in Court circles). He felt that there was something pre-ordained and universally valid about the titles of respect which were bestowed upon him. Where most painters of a later day agree with Cocteau that "It is not enough to *refuse* the Legion of Honour: the important thing is never to have deserved it," Reynolds in the last year of his life put it on record that "Distinctions are what we all seek after, and the world does set a value upon them, and I go with the great stream of life."

This was a point of view which permeated everything that Reynolds did in public. In private he might make jokes about horses pissing, and he might note of the catalogue to one foreign collection that it was "not worth a fart"; but in the *Discourses* he reminded his hearers that "it was said of Virgil that he threw even the dung about the ground with an air of dignity." He was a lifelong accommodator who in every situation sought to ease and lubricate, and although he himself was almost unnaturally well-behaved he had a taste for the company of people like Wilkes and Boswell who were very much less circumspect than himself. He could have portrayed his friends with the kind of undressed eloquence which Daumier and Degas were to deploy in the next century. But his familiar vision of John Wilkes was reserved for a rapid sketch in his appointment-book, while his portrait of Boswell in the National Portrait Gallery has little of the private face about it. It should be said, also, that his friends did not encourage him to be too free with their persons: "He may paint himself as deaf as he pleases," said Dr. Johnson, "but I will not be blinking Sam."

In this way it came about that Reynolds gave to his grand formal portraits the wide knowledge of the old masters which he ought, on his own reckoning, to have given to history-painting. The history which he honored was, that is to say, the history of the superior beings with whom he was privileged to come into contact. Looking at *The Death of Dido,* in the Queen's collection, or at the *Infant Academy* in Kenwood House, or at the *Theory* which he painted for the ceiling of the Royal Academy library, we see that they are better, but not all that much better, than Angelica Kauffmann's *Composition* or Northcote's *Jael and Sisera*. When we have said that *Theory* is a Titianesque variant after the *Mars* of Raphael, in S. Maria del Popolo in Rome, and that Reynolds may be presumed to have worked from an engraving by Nicolas Dorigny, we have said almost all that can be said in its favor. It could even be argued that as an image of concentrated effort the Kauffmann is more telling: Reynolds' notion of Theory is really too disheveled for his own tidy procedures.

These are, in fact, academic paintings in the dull, ineffective sense of the word. That "academic" can bear a better meaning is proved by Reynolds the portraitist. When he based his portrait of the 5th Earl of Carlisle on an amalgam of Veronese and the Apollo Belvedere it might have looked

Reynolds' arch mythologizing of his society of artists: *The Infant Academy*. Kenwood House, London.

Reynolds' grand formal style: *Georgiana, Duchess of Devonshire;* Reynolds had painted her as a child with her mother and later with her own daughter.

Reynolds' *Theory*, painted for the
ceiling of the Royal Academy, London.

Angelica Kauffmann's *Composition*, 1779-80, painted for
the Royal Academy's Lecture Room. Burlington House, London.

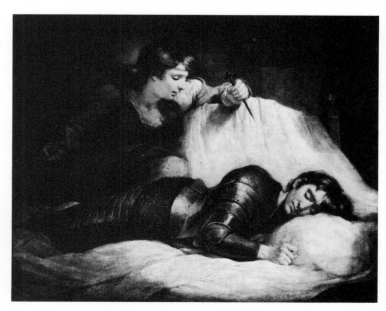

James Northcote, a history painter who began as Reynolds' assistant,
mastered his master's theories in such works as *Jael and Sisera*.

In Reynolds' *Three Graces Adorning a Term of Hymen*, 1774, society sisters reenact an antique phallic rite carefully shrouded in flowers. National Gallery, London.

Reynolds' *Cupid as a Link Boy*, consciously in the classic tradition of erotic symbolism. Albright-Knox, Buffalo. See colorplate p. 16.

Sir Joshua, P.R.A.

stilted and toadyish: but it didn't, because Reynolds knew how to fuse the two elements and to deliver, at the same time, an independent verdict on a pretty, spoiled, self-regarding young man who had just turned 21. This was the real argument, nowhere advanced in the *Discourses,* for an allusive art: that the allusions could be made to bounce in a new way. A supreme example of this, lately analyzed by E. H. Gombrich in his *Norm and Form,* is the *Three Graces Adorning a Term of Hymen* of 1773. This is, in fact, a *summa* of Reynolds' procedures as a portraitist. The learned and manifold allusions to earlier art, the regard for an exact likeness in the faces depicted and the unfailing blandness of the basic metaphor (note, for instance, how the garland is disposed to mask the phallus which, in one of the source-images, stood straight and firm on the hymeneal figure). This is not simply a learned painting: it is an allegory of the good life as it was lived by a favored few. Reynolds' own self-portrait in the R.A. is another allegory of that life: wearing the robes of his honorary Doctorate at Oxford, with a bust of Michelangelo at his side and the ms. (can it be?) of a discourse in his hand, the old gentleman seems to tick off, one after another, the constituents of happiness. (Quite other is, by the way, the quizzical, meticulous, hard-of-hearing figure of the President as he appears in Zoffany's group-portrait of His Majesty's Academicians, posing a male model.)

It was natural that envious people should see only the continual borrowings and be deaf to the bourdon of deep feeling which wells up in the great portraits. When Nathaniel Hone ridiculed Reynolds in his *The Conjuror* in 1775 he implied that Reynolds was an ingenious old faker who leafed through his collection of engravings, took what suited his purpose and served up the result as his own. But Reynolds was not concocting those pictures to score an unworthy triumph over his colleagues. He conceived them, wittingly or not, as magical objects which would show how the conditions of life could be transformed. People did not always live up to them: a classic instance is that of the double portrait of the Rev. George Huddesford and J. C. W. Bampfylde (1779), which celebrates an ideal of friendship which was soon to founder. But fundamentally the world of Reynolds' portraits is one in which the Old Masters say "Yes" in unison to the England of 1760-80. Reynolds would have died for the old masters, and he would have died for the England which made him unequivocally welcome: he got the two to work together in an unblemished harmony, but it was a harmony that sounded for him alone. It would be an exaggeration to say that the Royal Academy, as he conceived it, was an academy of one; but the concept of an academic art, as formed and put into practice by Sir Joshua, died with him and has never been resuscitated.

A Reynolds masterpiece: *George Huddesford and John Bampfylde,* 1779 (49¼ inches high), gifted young friends of Reynolds. National Gallery, London.

Johann Zoffany's *The Life Class at the Royal Academy,* 1772: Zoffany is at the extreme left; behind him, West; Reynolds is at the center with his ear-trumpet; Angelica Kauffmann is present only in her portrait in a rectangular frame—the women members of the Academy were not allowed to attend classes working from the live model. Windsor Castle.

V

Teutons in Togas

By Gert Schiff

Gert Schiff received his doctorate from the University of Cologne
and now teaches art history at Washington Square College, New York
University. His complete *catalogue raisonné* of the work of Henry
Fuseli will be published soon in Switzerland. He has written
articles on Fuseli, Blake, Gustave Moreau, Beckford and James Joyce.
This essay is dedicated to Richard Krautheimer on his 70th birthday.

There is at least one common feature in the art and lives of
Anton Raphael Mengs, Asmus Jakob Carstens, Peter Cornelius, Julius Schnorr von Carolsfeld, Anselm Feuerbach,
Arnold Böcklin and Hans von Marées: it was in Italy, and
mostly in Rome, that their art matured and their artistic
destinies were fulfilled. Besides, it may be said that they
were all "idealists" as opposed to "realists," insofar as they
endeavored to render lofty conceptions of the nature of man
in classicizing figural idioms.

But in making such a statement, we are already ensnared
in the ambiguities of art historical terminology. All these
artists were deeply affected by the Mediterranean ideals of
clarity of form, harmony and beauty; they all believed, to
varying degrees, in the absolute prëeminence of Greek art.
Some of them won international fame, some were admired
only by a few cultivated individuals, but in each case these
admirers believed that it was "their" artist who "preserved
the divine vision [i.e., the classical heritage] during times of
trouble." Yet, to modern eyes, Mengs is hardly more than a
late Baroque eclectic; Cornelius and Schnorr seem merely
historicizing illustrators working in the monumental genre;
Feuerbach's classical world appears un-archeological, natu-
ralistic and yet idealized; Böcklin's mythologies are natural-
istic without any attempt at idealization. Through a strict

Left: Frescoes in the Zoological Station at Naples by
Hans von Marées, whose grasp of pictorial concerns and
disregard for "historicizing" or even biographic detail
marks one of the most original of the German artists in Rome.

adherence to the linear style of neo-Attic reliefs, Carstens
came at times as close to the Greek ideal in style as, nearly
a hundred years later, Hans von Marées, without any re-
course to classical models, came close to it in spirit. But are
these artists to be considered as "academic"? Mengs, Cornelius and Schnorr acted successfully as directors of academies; Carstens and Böcklin each taught one or two years,
but only reluctantly; when Feuerbach was appointed to the
Vienna Academy, he was exhausted by the strains of his
career and was soon driven away by adversities. Marées
never had any connection with the world of official art and
its institutions. At the same time, he is the only one in this
line of artists who got beyond "academicism" in a broader
sense of the word. If we consider as "academic" those artists
whose development towards an authentic form of their own
is hampered by a dependence on the art or the spirit of a
past age, all the others were indeed academic.

Mengs (1728-1779) is generally credited with the creation
of the Neo-Classical style in painting, and his *Parnassus*
(1761), a ceiling painting in the Villa Albani, Rome, is
considered the key monument to this new artistic creed.
The contemporary fame of this work is as hard for us to
understand as its maker's ensuing reputation and influence.
Like everything in Mengs's œuvre, with the sole exception
of his portraits, *Parnassus* appears as the outcome of a
strained intellectual effort, and such was the whole career
of this artist. Mengs's father, painter to the court of the
Elector of Saxony in Dresden, wanted his son to become the
pictorial genius of the age; by naming him after Raphael
and Correggio, he predestined him to eclecticism. When he

Raphael Mengs's inaugural work of the Neo-Classic creed, a ceiling painting in the Villa Albani, Rome: *Parnassus*, 1761; his eclectic formula joining the Antique to High Renaissance models dominated the esthetics at German academies.

Teutons in Togas

took him to Rome for the first time in 1741-44, the boy was shut up every day for hours in the stanze of the Vatican in order to copy Raphael's murals. Four years later he became court painter himself, but faced with the task of painting a great altarpiece, Mengs felt he could carry it out only in Rome. And there he stayed; in 1754 he became director of the Roman Academy on the Capitoline Hill.

A few years later he met another newcomer from Dresden, Johann Joachim Winckelmann. Even as a child, this daemonic son of a poor cobbler in the backward Prussian county of Uckermark had been possessed by a burning love for antiquity. Despite his extreme poverty, he found the means to train himself thoroughly in the classical languages. In his first published work, *Reflections Concerning the Imitation of the Greek Works in Painting and Sculpture* (1775), Winckelmann outlined a whole program for a renewal of the arts based on the model of the ancients. He had founded his argument, however, almost exclusively on what he had read about Greek painting and sculpture in Pausanias, Pliny, etc., as there were hardly any antiquities to be seen in Dresden, where he drafted his pamphlet. At 40, Winckelmann came to Rome. He studied the monuments avidly; in his celebrated descriptions of the Laocoön, the Antinöus, the Apollo and the Torso Belvedere, he created a new mode of writing about art, and he seized the first opportunity to see and publish the excavations in Pompeii and Herculaneum. In 1764 he presented the learned world with an astonishing pioneer work: his *History of Antique Art,* a book which derived its competence from the author's wide reading, its life from his sensitive and sensuous response to the various manifestations of classical beauty. Winckelmann's whole interpretation of Greek and Roman art was centered

around its "classicalness," and that meant to him its static, harmonious, lovely features: witness his famous basic formula of "noble simplicity and tranquil grandeur." Winckelmann himself acknowledged that Mengs had given him great assistance in the technical part of his *History;* Mengs, on the other hand, found some of his dearest convictions endorsed by Winckelmann's theories—and thus, he believed, by the authority of the Ancients. Already in his early pamphlet Wickelmann stated that the "brush the artist wields must be dipped in intellect." In the *History of Antique Art,* he maintained as an axiom that "expression detracts from beauty." Beauty, according to Winckelmann, should be "a figure belonging neither to this nor to that particular person and not expressing any state of mind or feeling of passion, because these mingle foreign elements with beauty and disturb the unity." Such were the ideas which, out of their daily discussions, entered also into Mengs's own *Considerations on Beauty and Taste in Painting* (1762), a book that has rightly been called the "New Testament of Eclecticism," as it established the rule that the artist should follow Raphael for design, Titian for color, Correggio for grace—and the Ancients for general perfection. *Parnassus* must be viewed against the background of this esthetic.

In one important respect, this painting broke away from the prevailing tradition of ceiling decoration: it is not painted *"di sotto in su"* like those many painted apotheoses of the Baroque age which lead the eye in unbroken spatial continuity beyond the limits of the actual interior and finally into Heaven. Instead, Mengs constructed his *Parnassus* like an easel painting, as if the scene represented were viewed by a beholder almost at the same level with the figures. He thus renounced every theatrical illusion and presented his composition as a self-contained entity whose perspective construction bears no relation to its architectural setting. Yet, strangely enough, he was not even consistent in this bold demonstration of Neo-Classical rationalism for, in two side medallions, he painted the goddess of Rome, and Fame with the Plastic Arts, all hovering in clouds and seen from below.

Parnassus shows an Apollo who poses in the same attitude as *Theseus on Crete* in a Pompeian painting which had just been published. Some of the Muses around him, especially those of the Dance and of Lyric Poetry on the left, are equally inspired by Pompeian models; famous Roman beauties of the day, including Mengs's own wife, posed for some of the others. To Winckelmann this work represented "Antiquity reborn": its unprecedented perfection would make even Raphael bow his head, could he but see it. The figure of Apollo (which shows how easily the ideal of impassive beauty can degenerate into sloppiness) appeared to him as "Praxitelean"; in particular he found the painting of his knees unsurpassable. Among other excellences he noted the inclusion of a tenth figure, the one on Apollo's right, with her hand at her ear, which is the gesture of remembrance. She represents Mnemosyne, goddess of memory, who rightfully finds her place in this assembly since, according to Plato, the Muses are the daughters of Memory! Such exactitude pleased the learned antiquarian who, on the other hand, took offense at the fact that in Raphael's *Parnassus,* Apollo anachronistically plays a violin. To a present-day viewer, Mengs's *Parnassus* suffers from two shortcomings: its general anemia and its lack of a thoroughgoing compositional rhythm. The figures seem to have been conceived separately with gestures expressive of the arts they personify, and then pieced together. The brush "dipped in intellect" has been unable to create that kind of beauty which "belongs neither to this nor to that particular person" but unites them all in a lively unison. Yet this painting inaugurated a movement which, with the Homeric paintings of the Scot Gavin Hamilton, with the early works of Benjamin West, with the marble reliefs of Thomas Banks and the superficially classicizing amorous trifles of Joseph-Marie Vien (J.-L. David's teacher) soon spread throughout Europe.

Mengs died two decades later, exhausted by the hopeless struggle to emulate Tiepolo in his ceiling frescoes in the Royal Palace of Madrid, and Winckelmann was killed by a robber in an inn at Trieste as early as 1768. But in Germany, the esthetics of Mengs and Winckelmann survived their authors and remained uncontested for a long time, reinforced as they seemed to be by the theories of Lessing who, in his *Laocoön,* also held that expression in painting and sculpture should always be sacrificed to beauty. When, between 1799 and 1805, Goethe arranged his famous art-competitions on mythological themes, he distributed praise and blame according to the same principles; the artistic results were—should one say inevitably?—meager. Such was an outsider's view of Winckelmann's impact on the artistic culture of the Germans: in 1820, Henry Fuseli, the Swiss-born Keeper of the Royal Academy in London, wrote in the Introduction to

his *Lectures on Painting:* "Winckelmann was the parasite of the fragments that fell from the conversations or the tablets of Mengs. He reasoned himself into frigid reveries and Platonic dreams of beauty . . . To him Germany owes the shackles of her artists, and the narrow limits of her aims; from him they have learnt to substitute the means for the end, and by a hopeless chase after what they call beauty, to lose what alone can make beauty interesting: expression and mind." It took more than a century for Winckelmann's view of the Greeks to be finally superseded by the more catholic one which Friedrich Nietzsche set forth in *The Birth of Tragedy out of the Spirit of Music* (1870-71). To Nietzsche, the classical, "Apollonian" element so dear to Winckelmann is only one pole of the Greek sensibility; it is complemented by its anti-classical, "Dionysian" counterpart. Consequently, the nature of Greek art is determined by a tension between these poles, between harmony and ecstasy; self-knowledge and self-abandon; sculpture and music—beauty and expression. The future author of *Thus Spake Zarathustra* left no doubt as to his belief that the profoundest revelations, in art as in life, are to be found in the Dionysian realm. But it was only in twentieth-century Expressionism and Surrealism that the seed of his thought bore artistic fruit.

Yet there was at least one German artist who, during his final period in Rome in the 1790s, raised his art above the level of Mengsian eclecticism: Asmus Jakob Carstens (1754-98). Proud, uncompromising and impassioned, this son of a miller in a village near Schleswig had undergone much hardship before he was finally appointed a teacher of design at the Academy in Berlin. He used this office mainly for the realization of a lifelong dream: to obtain a scholarship and go to Rome, where he arrived in 1792. His own practice was opposed to the methods of academic teaching, which consisted in leading the student gradually from the copying of antique plaster casts to drawing from the nude. As a Platonist, Carstens believed in the superiority of imagination and ideas over visual perception; consequently he never drew from life, nor even from antique statues, rather he

A German Neo-Classic in Rome with a personal re-creation of Antiquity in somber Michelangelesque allegories: A. J. Carstens' drawing, *Night with Her Children Sleep and Death,* 1795. Schlossmuseum, Weimar.

studied the latter intensely for many hours and then drew them from memory. Hence he was only too happy when in Rome, released from the drudgery of the life-class, he could immerse himself in the marvels of ancient art and, soon, of Michelangelo as well. From the beginning he put his observations to use in a number of most original compositions. Summoned back after his two years of leave were over, he wrote to his well-intentioned patron, the Prussian Minister of Education, a wildly defiant letter. Not only was he resolved to stay—at the Academy's expense—but he also denounced the whole system of academies and the one in Berlin in particular as tyrannical and materialistic: he did not belong to the Berlin Academy but to mankind, which had a right to demand from him only the highest possible cultivation of his talents. Nowhere else but in Rome could he educate himself.

And this he did. Deprived of financial support, Carstens worked hard. His health was soon undermined by endless vigils, and he had to face an early death from consumption; what kept him alive was his immense will-power and the admiration of his friend and later biographer, the art critic Carl Ludwig Fernow. Most of Carstens's works were meant as designs for monumental frescoes which he was never to carry out. He depicted Jove crushing the rebellious Titans, based on the compositional pattern of Michelangelo's *Last Judgment* and obviously meant for a wall of the same dimensions. If he chose noble and pathetic subjects from Homer, like *Priam in the Tent of Achilles,* he rendered them in a graphic idiom which owed its rigidity to some neo-Attic reliefs or Greek vase paintings. The result—powerful figures full of subdued passion, viewed in pure profile

or frontally and set into a carefully constructed box space —breathed in every inch that "noble simplicity and tranquil grandeur" which Mengs never achieved. But Carstens also sought in the ancient writers, especially in Lucian, for subjects which corresponded to his own disillusioned and embittered view of the world. The story of *The Battle of the Philosophers* who, at the banquet of Aristaneitos, used their fists in support of their doctrines of detachment, self-denial and peace, appealed to this hater of academies. When the French Revolution was at its height, Carstens chose among Lucian's *Dialogues of the Dead* the "democratic" tale of *Megapenthes* as a subject for various large compositions. Summoned to Hades by Hermes, this slovenly young tyrant was unwilling to give up his sweet life. While the souls were embarking for their crossing of the Acheron, Megapenthes escaped but was caught and brought back by an old cobbler and a cynic philosopher; he had to lay down his insignia on the shore, was chained to the mast and the cobbler sat on his neck. In his drawing of the crowd on board, Carstens attempted to render the "dregs" of ancient society as if he had wanted to teach his contemporaries that the new tyranny from below was as bad as the old tyranny from above. He drew heavily on statues of satyrs and Roman actors, and on the well-known type of Silenus, in short, on the whole realm of the grotesque in Hellenistic and Roman sculpture. He thus derived anti-classical features directly from the antique.

But Carstens was greatest in compositions of a metaphysical character. Here his striving after ultimates and his melancholy combined in truly striking images. In an elaborate drawing of *The Birth of Light* (after an obscure Phoenician mythographer, Sanchoniathon), he came surprisingly close to Blake's contemporaneous illustrations of his own cosmology (e.g. *The First Book of Urizen,* 1794). Among similar works, one stands out clearly for its enigma and deep emotional impact: *Night with Her Children, Sleep and Death,* 1795. Carstens' pencil drawing is the first exact rendering of a celebrated passage in Hesiod's *Theogony* about Night who, at the beginning of time, gave birth to Fate, the Parcae, Nemesis, Sleep, Death and a number of other beings. The artist had been introduced to Greek mythology by Karl Philipp Moritz, a scholar who held the view that the fables of the Greek gods contained hidden traces of the world's primeval history: this determined Carstens' own treatment of those cosmological characters—not as allegorical personifications, but as living creatures with blood in their veins and with marked individual characters. He designed a gloomy cave, image of the archetypal womb. In the background, the hooded figure of Fate holds the book of human destiny out of which the three sisters sing the song of Life: Clotho sings the past; Lachesis, while singing the present, spins out the thread which Atropos, with the tune of futurity on her lips, is ready to cut with her shears. Next to them Nemesis is seated; her posture recalls that of Michelangelo's Delphic Sibyl. She looks aside; the expression of her tight lips is relentless, almost sour; she holds a cat-o'-nine-tails, for she *is* the scourge of mortals, checking

Friedrich Overbeck's *Italia and Germania,* 1811-28 (41 inches high; Pinakothek, Berlin) is complexly symbolic: of an idealized bond with his friend Franz Pforr and, ultimately, of the Nazarene hope of submitting Latin beauty to German inwardness. See colorplate p. 60.

Cornelius' weird masterpiece fuses the Gothic of Dürer with Classic Greece: *Apocalyptic Riders,* drawing, ca. 1850. National Gallery, Berlin.

Cornelius' contribution to the Nazarenes' revival of fresco painting reveals his ripening under the impact of Italian Renaissance art: *Joseph Interprets Pharaoh's Dreams,* 1816. National Gallery, Berlin.

Cornelius' vision of the "secret Christianity" of the Greeks is expressed in this cartoon for his frescoes in the Munich Glyptothek: *Aphrodite and Eros Rescuing Paris,* 1825. National Gallery, Berlin.

their pride and hubris, bestowing punishment and reward according to just measure, chastising hidden evil. And all these agitated figures surround one sublimely harmonious group. Like a Madonna of Mercy, Night holds her garment draped over her widespread arms and shows, wrapped in it and leaning against her knee, her two sleeping children, the harbingers of peace. Significantly, only the child who personifies sleep is represented slumbering fast and completely relaxed, with poppies gliding out of his hand; "Death," with his torch turned to the ground, sleeps standing, with a troubled face as if unable ever to rest. The viewer is not presented with an allegorical tableau vivant, as in Mengs's *Parnassus,* but with a glimpse of the eternal powers behind life.

The next scene in this "Pilgrimage to the Unattainable," as one might aptly summarize the pursuits of the German painters in Rome, was enacted by a group of painters commonly called the "Nazarenes." A handful of students of the Academy in Vienna, headed by Friedrich Overbeck and Franz Pforr, found themselves in opposition to the spirit and the methods of this institution and in 1809, they formed a group, the "Brotherhood of St. Luke." Their program was a renewal of Christian art based on the stylistic principles and the "innocent" spirit of German Gothic and Italian quattrocento painting. They moved to Rome, established themselves in an old monastery and soon attracted to their circle a great many of the most gifted young German artists, including Peter Cornelius and Julius Schnorr von Carolsfeld. A retrospective movement thus united Germany's avant garde; although it must be admitted that the crisp, archaizing, stridently-colored early paintings by Pforr and Overbeck were certainly much more original and even vital than anything the outlived tradition of Mengsian Neo-Classicism could still produce. Rome which, thanks to Winckelmann, Mengs, J.-L. David, Carstens, Canova and Thorwaldsen, had been for more than half a century the stronghold of the revival of antiquity, became now the somewhat less appropriate stage of a revival of the Christian Middle Ages. The German promoters of this new trend soon considered themselves the only true heirs to the Eternal City's spiritual and artistic legacy. They believed that the union of Latin beauty and German inwardness, consummated in a truly

Christian spirit, would unfailingly bear the fruit of another Renaissance. Overbeck's painting of *Italy and Germany*—personifications of the two countries, with their hands joined and their foreheads leaning against each other—gave expression to this hopeful vision. However, in the minds of the Nazarenes, the innate German longing for the South was combined with a peculiar insensitivity to the fullness and sensuous beauty of Southern life. Although almost everybody within the orbit of the Nazarenes became a Roman Catholic—a few, like Overbeck, out of profound spiritual necessity; many others merely out of intellectual snobbism—in their hearts and minds and, alas! also in their art, there remained all too much Protestant puritanism. True, the young Schnorr von Carolsfeld could once write that, as far as he was concerned, he liked much better "the sight of a beautiful Albanese on her mule than the sight of Frau Höhn aus Schönfeld with her basket, herself a beast of burden, as

Unlike Cornelius, Schnorr von Carolsfeld failed to regain a visionary basis for his art after the Nazarenes left
Rome: here, a theatrical battle scene from his encyclopedic *Nibelungen* frescoes, 1831-42. Royal Palace, Munich.

Teutons in Togas

it were." But one cannot miss the note of condescension in his concluding formula of the "vivid, sensuous, basically childlike manner" of the Italians—the "soulless, false Italians," as he calls them in another letter. Later on when the art of the Nazarenes had won serious recognition in Rome as well as the enthusiastic partisanship of the Bavarian Crown Prince, Schnorr's and the whole group's national egotism reached an almost incredible peak of naïve insolence: "The real, true Rome belongs to us. Had it depended on us, we would have crowned the Prince King of Rome and chased the Italians out of the temple!" Even in Overbeck's symbolic painting, Germania's attitude expresses both eager courting and gentle instruction; her brunette sister submits.

Indeed, the activities of this group form a strangely inconsistent interlude in the artistic history of Rome. Completely unassimilated to the Italian way of life, the Nazarenes failed also in their attempts at integrating their Italian models into their art. Despite their frequent borrowings from the quattrocento and Renaissance masters, including Raphael, their style was, in its essence, a derivation from the art of Dürer and his circle, filtered through a particular kind of linear asceticism. Like every other group or community of artists, the Nazarenes encompassed a great variety of talents and temperaments; needless to say they did not create a collective style, but worked in a variety of eclectic idioms.

Their art appears at its purest in their drawings: these include meticulous yet unified views of the landscape around Rome (especially their favorite spot, Olevano), penetrating portraits, and beautifully chaste nudes. A number of Nazarene drawings, especially those of Schnorr, are certainly among the finest ever done by German artists.

Among their religious paintings there are a few small ones which really breathe a pristine innocence of feeling. But as with most Romantic artists, the Nazarenes' innermost aim was a renewal of monumental painting. On two occasions, in 1816-17 and again in 1822-32, certain members of the group were given opportunities to paint large murals. For the second and more important of these cycles, the Casino Massimo frescoes, I must refer to Keith Andrews' excellent monograph on the Nazarenes, the first comprehensive study of the movement in the English language. There, a number of colored reproductions and an extensive commentary introduce the reader to those vivid depictions of episodes from Tasso, Ariosto and Dante which Overbeck, Schnorr and Führich, Veit and Koch respectively painted on the walls and ceilings of three rooms in the garden house of the Massimi family, near the Lateran church. The Casino Massimo is well worth a visit by the seriously interested.

The earlier frescoes are no longer *in situ* but can be viewed in the National Gallery in Berlin. Commissioned by the

Prussian Consul General in Rome, S. J. Bartholdy, for a room in his residence, the Palazzo Zuccari, they illustrate the Old Testament story of Joseph in Egypt. The artists involved were Overbeck, Philipp Veit, Wilhelm Schadow and, above all, Peter Cornelius.

Cornelius (1783-1867) was the son of the superintendent of the Düsseldorf Gallery; hence he absorbed a rich artistic and predominantly classical culture. Born a Roman Catholic, he was spared the inner struggles and the excesses of religious zeal or bigotry which characterized the many converts in the group. Even in his youth, Cornelius described his own artistic character as "glowing and severe" (*glühend und streng*). His career began with not very successful contributions to Goethe's art competitions. The next stage of his development was formed by three series of drawings illustrating Goethe's *Faust,* the *Nibelungenlied* and *Romeo and Juliet.* In these, the Neo-Classical linear style of his beginnings was enlivened by expressive, crisp and convoluted forms derived from the graphic art of Dürer. When Cornelius entered the circle of the Nazarenes, his art ripened further under the impact of Italian art. Giotto led him back to an essential clarity of form; Masaccio made him aware of the problems of plastically articulated figures in space. In his striving after dramatic representation, Cornelius was the first of the Nazarenes to find his way from the early, Peruginesque Raphael (upon whose model most of the others based their styles) to the master of the tense and agitated scenes in the Vatican frescoes.

All this can be seen in his painting of *Joseph Interpreting Pharaoh's Dreams,* in the Casa Bartholdy frescoes. As has often been noticed, the composition is only distantly related to the identical scene in Raphael's cycle in the Loggie. Cornelius contrasts the quiet, erect figure of Joseph with the group of courtiers who react to his interpretations with expressions of doubt, malice, astonishment and awe. The distant landscape has a graphic distinctiveness reminiscent of early Renaissance painting. The medallions with representations of the Years of Plenty and the Lean Years of the dreams seem deliberately archaic.

Originally Cornelius was commissioned to paint the Dante room in the Casino Massimo. He had already made a design for the ceiling, depicting the *Paradiso,* when in 1819 the newly crowned King Ludwig I of Bavaria called him to Munich in order to execute murals on a much larger scale. At the same time he was invited to become Director of the new Academy in his native Düsseldorf. Cornelius accepted both offers.

His first task in Munich was to paint frescoes in the Glyptothek, Leo von Klenze's building for the royal collection of ancient art. Naturally these frescoes had to deal with the gods and heroes of antiquity, and Cornelius derived his program from Hesiod, Homer and Aeschylus. To his brother artists in Rome this was a disappointment. They, having rejected the classical world in favor of Christian and patriotic-medieval subjects, could only regret that the first commission one of their circle received on native ground should compel him again to submit to this "reactionary" tradition.

Yet Cornelius attempted to deal with ancient mythology in a Christian spirit, or to disclose in the crucial myths the "secret Christianity" of the Greeks. Thus, Hercules rescuing Prometheus was meant as a symbol of the Savior; and Eros as the ruler of the elements, the seasons and the continents was to be understood as the love of God which permeates all creation. The destruction of Troy stood for man's disobedience, hubris and mutual hate. Cornelius felt himself here to be the heir of Carstens, who had brought classical mythology to life again. Yet Carstens, as a classicist, had been concerned with the individual myths and their human content, whereas Cornelius as a Romantic sought for the inner unity and metaphysical significance of the whole of mythology (H. von Einem).

The Glyptothek and Cornelius' frescoes with it were destroyed during the last war; what survive are his large-size cartoons in charcoal on cardboard. It is easy to see that color added to such a design could be only incidental. Such, indeed, was the role of color in Cornelius' remaining works. It can even be said that for him the creative part of his painting consisted in designing his cartoons; their transposition to the walls was merely a duty. Or, in the words of Hermann Grimm: "Cornelius created his compositions only for the inner eye, as it were, just as our classical poets wrote their plays only for an ideal stage in whose existence they never believed."

After the Glyptothek, the King commissioned Cornelius to decorate Friedrich von Gärtner's Ludwigskirche in Munich. The painter worked out an elaborate scheme covering the whole of Biblical history from the Fall of the Rebel Angels to the Apocalypse, with Christ's redeeming sacrifice at the center; but he had to reduce it in scope as he was finally given only the walls and vaults of the presbyterium and crossing. Cornelius designed the cartoons in Rome, as henceforth he did with every important work. He needed the proximity of the works of Michelangelo and Raphael as well as the inspiring contact with Overbeck. In 1836-39 he painted without assistance the choir fresco of the *Last Judgment,* on a wall higher and deeper than the corresponding one in the Sistine Ceiling; but all his devotion did not suffice to imbue this elaborate theological allegory with life. The King was disappointed and withdrew his favor from the aging artist.

Cornelius, however, found a new patron in King Friedrich Wilhelm IV of Prussia, "the Romantic on the throne," whose innermost aim was to bridge the gulf between the Christian sects and to establish a universal church. This philosophic ruler responded to the artist's cherished idea of a great Christian fresco cycle. Cornelius was to carry it out on the walls of a projected Campo Santo adjacent to the rebuilt Berlin Cathedral. From 1843 on he worked on the cartoons, again mainly in Rome; and it is certainly a unique example of an artist's loyalty to his dream that, although the Revolution of 1848 swept away the whole project, Cornelius did not abandon the work but devoted the entire rest of his life, almost 20 years, to this series of gigantic charcoal drawings— in spite of the fact that there could never conceivably be any other place for them than in the storerooms of Berlin's National Gallery where they are to this day. Working thus in a complete void, the artist felt a supreme peace of mind. Since he had lost both public and patronage, he no longer had to care about execution, color or communicability; he could express his inner world, a world of subjective theological speculation, in his favorite medium which was as abstract as his thoughts. For him, these cartoons embodied the best of his powers; he believed that they would last a thousand years.

And in the first drawing at least, he created a weird masterpiece. *The Apocalyptic Riders* (ca. 1850), usually reproduced alone, but complete only with the predella depicting *The Seven Works of Mercy* and the crowning lunette showing *The Angels of Wrath,* is undoubtedly a work of great force. Apart from its obvious model, Dürer's woodcut of the same subject, it draws upon the example of Raphael's tapestry cartoons at Hampton Court and, allegedly, upon the sculptures of the Parthenon. It must have been thanks to the impact of Phidias that Cornelius rendered the four archenemies of mankind not as grim medieval ghosts in the vein of Dürer. Instead, Pestilence, Famine, War and Death seem almost of the same titanic breed as those they mow down. The woman who throws herself against the beautiful Apocalyptic Warrior seems to be struck by the recognition of a profound kinship, as though brothers were meeting each other on a battlefield. Destruction is shown here as the complement of life in the fulfillment of the Divine plan.

It is interesting to compare Cornelius' design with Schnorr's battlescene from his *Nibelungen* frescoes in the Royal Palace in Munich (1831-42). The difference between Cornelius as an illustrator of ideas and Schnorr as an illustrator of stories is obviously also a difference of quality. Despite Schnorr's sovereign handling of the fighting masses, his rendering of the death-struggle of the Burgundians seems staged and one feels it is only one step from here to the turgid history-painting of the Belgian school and its present-day continuation in Cinemascope.

Cornelius' isolation and the ensuing subjectivity of his art were due mainly to that radical change in the social consciousness which originated in the revolution of 1848. He had started out as an "official artist," sponsored by the ruling powers and intent on giving visible form to what he could still rightly consider the common creed and the common cultural heritage of the majority of his contemporaries. He wanted to complete a tradition which, according to him, was still incomplete and vital; consequently, he drew deliberately upon its visual correlate, the art of the past. In the case of that later-born German Roman, Anselm Feuerbach (1825-80), isolation and neglect were due to a primary incompatibility of his aims and ideals with the demands of his presumptive public, the new bourgeoisie. Aristocratic and escapist in character, his art grew out of his scornful contempt for the materialism, the lack of spiritual and esthetic orientation, the complacent efficiency of his contemporaries. So deliberately was he at variance with his time that, despite his lifelong complaints, his fate as an unappreciated genius appears almost self-imposed. For him, there were no public commissions; even later, when he was famous, his petition to paint the walls of the House of Parliament was turned down. No wonder he shared Nietzsche's pessimism regarding the cultural future of the new German Empire.

The soul of Feuerbach's art, his conception of a higher, nobler humanity, was an entirely subjective norm, quite distinct from that objective ideal of classical beauty which Mengs, Carstens and even Cornelius still sought in the Greeks. Consequently Feuerbach found the visible resources for his image of man not in statues and reliefs, but among Italy's men and women, in the unaffected *grandezza* of their race. His eclecticism was thus of a different kind. For eclectic he was, and the master who had led him along the road of eclecticism was Thomas Couture, who is still remembered for his *Romans in the Period of Decadence* (1847). Feuerbach was certainly not affected by the particular gift Couture displayed in this painting: the art of being piquant, but inoffensive. But he was affected by Couture's praise of Veronese and Tiepolo as models for large-scale historical compositions, and by his buff, blue-green and yellow tonality. Couture's little-known portrait of the young Feuerbach as a graceful, narcissistic shepherd (1852-53) bears witness to their association.

Later in Italy, Feuerbach turned from Tiepolo and Veronese to Titian, Raphael and, to a lesser extent, to the antique. But it was only when he met his model, Nana Risi, in 1860, that he became psychologically free for the realization of vision. This uneducated girl from Trastevere, a "noble animal" with the looks of a ripe princess, possessed that "truly majestic, forbidding tranquillity" which Feuerbach needed. He painted her as Bianca Cappello, Lucrezia Borgia, Iphigenia, Medea and, many times, as herself. Quite often these arresting portraits really convey something of that deeper harmony between man and life which Feuerbach opposed to the restlessness of his age. But his was an elusive ideal. In his history paintings he never achieved that "even penetration of the idealist and the realist elements" which was his esthetic aim. Invariably they express not an action, but its suspension, or a mood, mostly a longing. So, in his *Judgment of Paris* (1870) the shepherd arbiter appears inert as if, in a reverie on the essence of beauty, he had lost sight of the living beauty he is supposed to judge. With the flocks of *amorini,* a particular period prettiness sneaks into the painting. Their games are as incompatible with the elegiac mood of the scene as this mood itself is incompatible with the concept of Classicism. Out of sheer *horror vacui* the artist has filled every empty spot with their fluttering presence, so that he himself for once appears prone to that restlessness and lack of esthetic orientation which he so sharply denounced in his contemporaries.

In comparison *The Feast of Plato,* at least in its first, less ornamental version (1869), is still a great painting. Its striking archeological inaccuracy (e.g. the absurd, almost Makart-like wall-paintings, the interlocutors sitting around a table instead of reclining on couches) seems justified as it only indicates that the painter's aim was not to render the historical banquet of Agathon but, again, its mood and that lasting

The ultimate eclecticism of a German Roman, Anselm Feuerbach: *Medea*, 1870 (77¾ inches high); the star is Nana Risi, a "noble animal" important to his painting both as model and inspiration. Bayerische Staatsgemäldesammlungen, Munich.

Feuerbach's *Judgment of Paris*, 1870: Classicism is travestied by prettiness and by the destruction of an elegiac mood implied in the fluttering presences of the *amorini*. Kunsthalle, Hamburg.

The Feast of Plato, 1869 (116 inches high), is Feuerbach at his Neo-Classic best, both in the evocative mood and the sustained rationality of the composition; this despite the absurdity of the Pompeian decor. Staatliche Kunsthalle, Karlsruhe.

Arnold Böcklin's *Island of the Dead*, 1880 (43¾ inches high), in his famous allegorical style; its metaphysical aura influenced the Surrealists including both Chirico and Dali. Oeffentliche Kunstsammlung, Basel.

Teutons in Togas

aroma of wine, roses and burning torches which surrounded Alcibiades when, drunk and leaning upon his flute-players, he entered the house in search of Socrates. The spheres are clearly separated: on the right, we see the wise men, deeply involved in their argument; on the left, the revelers, headed by the politician and dandy who, with his exuberant gesture, pays the most fervent homage beauty ever paid to a great mind.

Viewed against Feuerbach's strained, hypersensitive, aristocratic nature, Böcklin (1827-1901) appears almost as an incarnation of robust middle-class energy. He, too, had to struggle for recognition, but he worked himself up with Germanic stubbornness, and although he had to endure much hardship, he was much less subject to self-pity and doubts. Politically he was no less conservative than Feuerbach and he shared this outlook, characteristically, with painters like Puvis de Chavannes, Gustave Moreau and Dante Gabriel Rossetti, who were all born between 1820 and 1830. Böcklin's witnessing of the bloodshed during the revolution of 1848 in Paris determined his Prussian-oriented monarchism—and his aversion to everything that was French in art and esthetics. Most of Böcklin's working life was spent in Florence and Rome.

His attitude toward painting underwent one decisive change: about 1856, he turned from a Corot-inspired, atmospheric conception of landscape in which the human fig-ure played only a subordinate role, to a certain kind of allegoric painting in which fabulous beings, personifications of the powers of nature, became predominant, and the landscape itself only accessory.

Böcklin's relation to antiquity was paradoxical. Although he derived much of his subject-matter from Greek mythology, he was not especially well versed in the classics and he did not care at all for historical accuracy. "The Ancients didn't want to make antiques either," he used to say. Yet it could happen that his purely imaginary design of a "Sanctuary of Hercules" was "verified" by later excavations. He never really studied ancient sculpture although he had very strong opinions as to its original polychromy. Pompeian painting impressed him deeply when he first saw it in 1862: it may have led him towards a greater emphasis on the tectonic element in his compositions; it certainly induced him to use brighter colors and, above all, to turn from oils to painting with tempera and encaustic with which he experimented all his life.

But the fauns, tritons, nereids and naiads who abound in his later paintings have certainly less to do with antiquity than with the artist's own experience of nature or—as noted by the late Georg Schmidt—with his experience of contemporary society and its attitude toward sex.

The *Naiads at Play*, 1886, is typical of Böcklin's complete renunciation of that kind of idealization which, it is commonly believed, can alone make mythological compositions credible. Were it not for their fish-tails, these creatures could well be taken for a group of unusually sportive visitors to a seaside resort. Indeed, the stately, red-haired naiad in the foreground is said to be the portrait of a highly respectable drawing teacher from Basle, and the middle-aged triton on her right looks really more like a Swiss notary than a son of Poseidon. What gives credibility to their extraordinary performance is the fact that they all betray in every movement the most genuine familiarity with, or the most complete mastery over, the element which is unmistakably theirs. And yet, the discord between their screaming vacation excitement and our conception of seagods remains as painfully unresolved as the contrast between the strikingly realistic painting of sea and rocks and the clashing purples and chrome-oranges of some of the naiads. A positivistic fairy-tale, embodying the pantheism of a boom period!

There is another aspect of Böcklin's art, exemplified by *The Island of the Dead* (1880). To many of us, this forbidding spot may look rather like a stage design (Richard Wagner thought that Böcklin, if only he wished, would be the ideal designer for his *Ring*). Yet Chirico derived from this painting some of the "mystery and melancholy" of his metaphysical cityscapes, and Dali took it as a model for his Surrealist transformations of the bay at Port Lligat.

With the art of Hans von Marées (1837-87), we finally enter a realm which is free from all those fatal contradictions which we found in the works of most of the others. Shortly before he painted his murals in the Marine-Zoological Station in Naples, he wrote to his friend, the art critic Konrad Fiedler: "I long for nothing more than the moment in which conception and representation will flow together to form a unity." Fiedler, with whom Marées traveled to Spain, France and Holland in 1869, supported him until the end of his life with an allowance. In his writings about the philosophy of art, he arrived at far-reaching conclusions: "The work of art does not imitate or transform reality, it produces reality. . . The work of art must replace Nature." Indeed, Fiedler's writings, as well as Marées' art, do not mark the end of the period under consideration, but a beginning of modernity.

Hans von Marées, the son of an old, distinguished family, was born in Elberfeld. Destined early to be a painter, he studied in Berlin and Munich and went to Italy in 1865. He spent almost all his life in this, his spiritual country. Marées remained unmarried and, apart from his lasting connection with Fiedler, his biography includes a few friendships with artists, especially the sculptor Adolf von Hildebrand. In his late years he had a few rather insignificant pupils. Relentless in his demands on himself as well as on others, harsh and uncompromising, extremely secretive about his inner life, Marées was predestined to loneliness. Under these conditions, he sustained throughout his life the almost superhuman effort which finally resulted in his great late style.

The frescoes in Naples, an earlier work, are the product of a particularly happy period in his life. In 1869, Marées met the naturalist Anton Dohrn who was then planning the foundation of the Marine-Zoological Station. When in 1873 the building with all its scientific inventory was ready, Dohrn invited Marées and Hildebrand to paint and decorate the walls of the central lecture room. Hildebrand's share was two portrait busts and the ornamental parts of the walls. From August until November, Marées worked in one continuous creative spurt. He had been used to working intermittently, with recurrent periods of discouragement, and hardly ever finishing anything. Now he invented the whole series almost at once and carried it out without much alteration, seemingly effortlessly. The speedy execution required by the fresco technique obviously helped him.

On the smaller west wall he painted two groups of nude fishermen who carry their nets and push their boat into the sea in front of two Capri-like rocks. The broad north wall is covered by a large seascape with a long, flat boat. Four powerful, sunburnt Neapolitans row a dreaming woman and an old man across the bay. Opposite, the south wall is subdivided by two windows giving on the terrace, but the fresco runs throughout. It depicts an orange grove; on the left we see two young women on a bench; on the right, two children, a youth who plucks an orange and an old man gardening. On the east wall Marées painted a strange ruined building with a pergola. This was a tavern in the neighborhood, favored by Marées' whole circle. And indeed we see, seated around the table in a corner beneath the stairs, first Dohrn, the founder of the Station, with a slightly weary expression; then, standing, the physiologist Kleinenberg; next to him John Grant, a sturdy Scottish bohemian; finally Marées and Hildebrand. On the stone banister sits Regina Giovanna, the innkeeper; at the extreme right, an oyster woman sits on the ground.

There are serious reasons for some critics' claim that these still little-known frescoes are the most accomplished work of

Arnold Böcklin's *Naiads at Play,* 1886, reveals a contradictory eclecticism in which Greek demi-gods frolic like healthy middle-class Germans at the beach. Oeffentliche Kunstsammlung, Basel.

mural painting in the nineteenth century. One of their strikingly new features is the absence of any "subject-matter" in the traditional sense. No story is told, no symbolism is concealed in these simple, everyday scenes. True, there is a faint trace of the old iconographic type of *The Ages of Man* in the right part of the orange grove, and one could even find a subconscious reminiscence of Overbeck's *Italy and Germany* in the two women on the left, although one feels rather uncomfortable in linking the older, didactic work with this fresco which is nothing but most intimately, most endearingly human. But then, all these everyday scenes are imbued with universal validity, most miraculously so in the case of the pergola fresco where the portrayal of the circle of friends seems to have been stripped, as it were, of all its immediate biographic reality—with the result that the group appears as an intense condensation of life. How has all this been achieved? We may point to the marvelous balance between the compositions and their architectural framework, between the figures and space, between the various spatial layers and the basic two-dimensionality of the frescoes. We may equally point to the fact that here the human figure is primarily treated as a formal element of the composition, as was the

rule in all great monumental art of the Mediterranean tradition. Furthermore, there are the colors, "autonomous" and yet true to the Neapolitan scene, colors which emanate light without rendering it. But there remains a considerable residue which can only be explained by the artist's genius, by his happy vision and by his deep experience of a fruitful and fateful hour.

And yet, it is still a far cry from these forceful achievements to the late works of Marées, above all his four great Triptychs. These, however, would rise so much above anything "academic" that they cannot be dealt with in the present context.

Among the various sources used for this article, the following should be mentioned:

A. Kamphausen: *Asmus Jakob Carstens, Neumuenster in Holstein*, 1941.
Keith Andrews: *The Nazarenes, A Brotherhood of German Artists in Rome*, Oxford, 1964.
Herbert von Einem: *Peter Cornelius*, Wallraf-Richartz Jahrbuch XVI, 1954.
Julius Meier-Graefe: *Hans von Marées*, Munich and Leipzig, 1909.

Among the most impressive little-known masterpieces of late 19th-century painting are Hans von Marées' frescoes of 1873 in the Zoological Station at Naples [left, below, right].

Friedrich Overbeck: *Italia and Germania*, 1811-28
(37 inches high). Neue Pinakothek, Munich. See page 50.

Arnold Böcklin: *The Honeymoon*, 1875 (25½ inches high).
Gottfried Keller Foundation, Berne, Switzerland.
See essay by Gert Schiff beginning on page 46.

60

James McNeill Whistler: *Rose and Silver: La Princesse
du Pays de la Porcelaine*, 1864 (78½ inches high).
Freer Gallery of Art, Washington, D.C. See
essay by Allen Staley beginning on page 80.

Jean-Léon Gérome: *Queen Rodope Observed by Gyges*, 1859
(26½ inches high). Museo de Arte, Ponce, Puerto Rico.
See essay by Gerald M. Ackerman beginning on page 100.

Jehan-Georges Vibert: *The Startled Confessor*, ca. 1880
(33¼ inches high). Metropolitan Museum, New York.
See essay by Thérèse Burollet beginning on page 88.

Frederick, Lord Leighton: *Flaming June,* 1895
(47½ inches square). Museo de Arte, Ponce, Puerto Rico.
See essay by Allen Staley beginning on page 80.

Jean-Auguste-Dominique Ingres: *The Dream of Ossian*
[detail], 1813. Musée Ingres, Montauban, France.
See essay by Robert Rosenblum beginning on page 67.

VI

Ingres, Inc.

By Robert Rosenblum

A professor at New York University's Institute of Fine Arts, Robert Rosenblum has published books on Cubism and on late eighteenth-century painting. His book on Ingres, which includes material in this essay, is published this fall by Harry N. Abrams.

In histories of nineteenth-century French art, the most respected and most unloved of Ingres' major paintings, the *Apotheosis of Homer,* has come to symbolize the official position which its master upheld throughout two-thirds of the century. Commissioned in 1826 as a ceiling decoration for the Louvre, the *Apotheosis* was intended to fix for all time a hierarchy of permanent classical values that could crush, from its Olympian heights, the contemporary assaults of the Romantic infidels as well as any future challenges to a familiar world of eternal beauty. Yet later generations have been able to see with growing clarity that Ingres' art is more complex and contradictory than this stubborn affirmation of classical faith against the changing values of nineteenth-century experience and that, in turn, the less official lessons learned from his paintings could inspire more wilfully modern artists from Degas, Renoir and Seurat to Matisse, Picasso and Gorky. And in his own time, the diversity of Ingres' art was reflected on less exalted levels by a host of students and academic followers who rephrased, with varying degrees of originality, the inventions of the master.

The *Apotheosis* itself established a pictorial canon of academic authority that soon reappeared, appropriately enough, in the hemicycle decorations of the Ecole des Beaux-Arts, where Ingres replaced Jean-Baptiste Regnault as professor on

December 30, 1829 and where, in 1833-34, he served as Vice-President and President. Completed in 1841 and signed in the following year, Paul Delaroche's enormous, semicircular mural, *Artists of All the Ages,* presides over this educational institution as Ingres' own *Apotheosis* was to preside over the Louvre. Consonant with its doctrinaire assertion of timeless values, its structure is inflexibly symmetrical, an encyclopedic compilation of 77 architects, painters and sculptors from the four great historical periods who take their places in front of an Ionic colonnade that centers upon a Holy Greek Trinity of Ictinus, Apelles and Phidias, who judge all posterity from their Jovian thrones.

However, such frozen emblems of classical supremacy were more the exception than the rule in Ingres' work as well as in that of artistic officialdom, and this rigidly didactic view of the lawgivers of classical truth and beauty could often be relaxed. Even Homer himself might be venerated in a manner less authoritative than Ingres' *Apotheosis,* witness only Jean-Baptiste-Auguste Leloir's Arcadian vision at the Salon of 1841, in which the greatest poet of them all is seated before a Doric temple in a primitive landscape, enchanting an enrapt audience of fellow Greeks with song and verse; and similarly, Ingres' other interpretations of the classical world could evoke experiences more beguiling and complicated than the unswerving allegiance to an absolute artistic deity in a century of perpetual revolution.

Thus, in the many versions of *Antiochus and Stratonice,* another kind of classical beauty is re-created, a beauty that conjures up a precious dream of late antiquity's Epicurean refinements. Like a miniature museum display of a Roman

Jean-Auguste-Dominique Ingres' *Madame Moitessier,* 1859 (58¼ inches high; National Gallery, Washington) is an almost perfect incarnation of the mid-nineteenth-century ideal of feminine beauty. See page 77.

to the master. For example, in *Comtesse d'Haussonville* (1845) or *Mme. Gonse* (1852), Ingres adapted the pose of a classical statue, Polyhymnia (which he also used for Stratonice), in which the sitter is seen supporting her chin and cheek with a delicately curled thumb and forefinger. The same gesture and classical allusion were rapidly echoed by lesser masters of portraiture, like Gérome and Ingres' own student Amaury-Duval, who transform the silent, enigmatic concentration of Ingres' female sitters, gazing mysteriously outward past the spectator, into a more prosaic mood of drawing-room coquetry. And even when Ingres borrows portrait formulas from his contemporaries or from his younger students, he elevated them to unexpected heights. Thus *Mme. Inès Moitessier* (1851) may well reflect such earlier paragons of flattering portraiture as Ary Scheffer's *Mme. Caillard* (1842) with its comparably fashionable mode of impeccably smoothed and polished hairline and bared shoulders, or his own student Hippolyte Flandrin's *Mme. Oudiné,* of 1840, with its strangely iconic symmetry that deifies the sitter as it would deify Ingres' *Madonna with a Crown.* Yet such sources are thoroughly absorbed in *Mme. Moitessier,* which transcends the prosaic vagaries of fashion in a nineteenth-century world of material grace and wealth and creates, rather, a haunting, timeless image of feminine grandeur and mystery, a secular goddess at whose shrine one could only worship. We can still understand today what Ingres' finest

critic, Théophile Gautier, meant when in 1847, on seeing the first studies of Ingres' other painted portrait of this lady, he described her beauty as Junoesque.

In general, Ingres' portraits of men coped more individually and candidly with the psychology of the sitter than did his portraits of women, which were usually altered more drastically to conform to preconceived nineteenth-century ideals of Olympian beauty and feminine charm; and in this, too, he was echoed by students and by later official portraitists. The directness of the early double-portrait drawing of two French architects in Rome, Leclère and Provost, is modestly paraphrased by Hippolyte Flandrin, whose 1835 double portrait of himself and his brother Paul belongs to the same early nineteenth-century world of intimate artistic brotherhoods. Ingres' portraits of more famous male personalities were no less acute in their revelations and no less important in creating portrait formulas to be used by other artists. There is, for one, the 1839 pencil drawing of Franz Liszt, whose covert passion and taut silhouette were quickly underscored in the following year by Ingres' student, Henri Lehmann, who painted the composer in 1840 with dual homage to Ingres' drawing and to the psychological intensity and shadowy drama of Delacroix's Romantic portraiture. More officially, too, Ingres managed to resurrect portrait prototypes that could ennoble the new aristocracy of a democratic century, as in his portrait of the Duc d'Orléans,

Ingres' *Mme. Moitessier* [left], 1851 (58½ inches high; National Gallery, Washington) transforms a popular kind of society portrait into a hymn to womanhood. Earlier, less inspired examples are Hippolyte Flandrin's *Mme. Oudiné,* 1840 (Lyons museum) and Ary Scheffer's *Mme. Caillard,* 1842 (Petit Palais, Paris).

which revives the compressed and frozen contours, the glossy surfaces, the haughty, attenuated poses of sixteenth-century Mannerist portraiture, and momentarily convinces the spectator that the pre-Revolutionary world of dukes, counts and kings somehow survived the assaults of history. His followers, however, could not maintain this artistic deception. Flandrin's portrait of Napoleon III at the Salon of 1863 repeats Ingres' paragon, but subtracts from it the icy tension of surface, the abstract precision of edge, leaving only a crowded inventory of imperial descriptive detail.

Indeed, for nineteenth-century officialdom, it was finally the literalism of Ingres' portraiture and of his art in general that triumphed. Consider only the fate of Ingres' portrait of the journalist Louis-François Bertin, a hypnotic amalgam of empirically studied physical and psychological realities and an abstractly invented network of sharp con-

tours and compressed volumes. In the same decade of the 1830s, this amalgam was already disintegrated by such other portraits of prominent political leaders under the Bourgeois King as that of Alexandre-Auguste Ledru-Rollin by Mme. Mongez; and by the end of the century (witness Léon Bonnat's portrait of the writer Ernest Renan in the year of his death, 1892), the vitality of *M. Bertin* could only be preserved in a most literal, photographic way. It would take a Picasso to resuscitate the psychic, physical and pictorial energy of this ghost, as he in fact was to do in his portrait of Gertrude Stein. But Picasso's many reincarnations of Ingres, like Seurat's, Matisse's or Gorky's, disclosed endlessly unofficial facets of the master's art, from precocious abstraction to Surrealist eroticism, facets that were inaccessible to nineteenth-century official painters as they were even to Ingres' own public consciousness as an artist and as an academician.

Ingres: *The Duke of Orléans*, 1844
(85⅞ inches high; Versailles museum).

Hippolyte Flandrin: *Napoleon III*,
Salon of 1863 (Versailles museum).

Ingres: *M. Bertin*, 1832 (45¾ inches high; Louvre).

Mme. Mongez: *Ledru-Rollin*, 1838 (Musée Carnavalet, Paris).

Bonnat: *Ernest Renan*, 1892 (Renan museum, Tréguier, France).

Picasso: *Gertrude Stein*, 1906 (Metropolitan, New York).

VII

The Condition of Music

By Allen Staley

A frequent contributor to art periodicals, Allen Staley wrote the
dissertation for his Yale Ph.D. on Pre-Raphaelite landscape
painting. He is on the staff of the Philadelphia Museum and is
currently working on a major exhibition of English art from 1760
to 1860, to be seen in Philadelphia and Detroit this season.

The first Impressionist exhibition took place in Paris in
1874. Three years later in London occurred an event of
almost equal significance for English art. This was the opening of the Grosvenor Gallery, which, by providing an opportunity to exhibit for artists who were not at home in the
Royal Academy, demonstrated what a large gap existed between the progressive painting in the capitals on either side
of the Channel. The immediate results of the Grosvenor
Gallery exhibition were the recognition of Edward Burne-
Jones as an artist of conspicuous significance, and Ruskin's
ill-tempered criticism of Whistler, which was to lead to their
famous libel suit. Both Whistler and Burne-Jones, as well
as the Grosvenor Gallery itself, represent aspects of a development in English art, which by the late 1870s was generally
called Aestheticism. As is often the case in England, this
movement was primarily literary; as early as 1868 Walter
Pater wrote an essay, "Aesthetic Poetry," about the verse of
William Morris; and *Patience,* Gilbert and Sullivan's lam-
poon of the movement, has as its hero Reginald Bunthorne
who is "greenery-yallery, Grosvenor Gallery," but a poet,
not a painter. Much of the painting, particularly that of
Burne-Jones, is literary in bias, Burne-Jones's medievalism
in paint corresponding to that of Morris in verse. However,
Burne-Jones represents only one stream of what properly

can be termed Aestheticism in painting. Running parallel is
another stream, classicizing rather than medievalizing, and
concerned with abstract and decorative rather than poetic
values. To this side of the movement belongs Whistler, but
it was practiced most consistently by Albert Moore.

Today, Moore is usually thought of in the light of Whistler. Born in 1841, he was Whistler's junior by seven years,
but nonetheless he had an influence at a crucial stage in
Whistler's development. Moore's paintings of the early 1860s
were of Biblical subjects painted in a style derived from
Holman Hunt and Ford Madox Brown; but in 1865 he
exhibited a painting at the Royal Academy, *The Marble
Seat,* showing classically draped figures seated in a landscape, which established a pattern he would follow for
the next 20 years. It also seems to have stimulated Whistler
to seek out its painter. They met in 1865 and became close
friends, so close that in 1866 Whistler wrote to Fantin-
Latour proposing that Moore should replace Alphonse Le-
gros as the third member of the "Society of Three" they had
founded to reform the world's art. In the following few
years their ambitions came into close harmony, as demonstrated by Moore's *Musician,* shown at the Royal Academy
in 1867, and Whistler's *Symphony in White, No. 4,* left un-
completed in the winter of 1868-69 or his so-called *Six
Projects* now in the Freer Gallery, Washington, D.C. In
1870 the similarity of their work even became a source of
contention between the two artists. They asked a mutual
friend, the architect W. Eden Nesfield, to arbitrate, and he
seems to have settled the matter to their mutual satisfaction:
"there is no harm in both painting in a similar way as the

Left: Women in Albert Moore's compositions of the '70s were pretexts
for color and pattern: even the titles *Birds* [far left] and *Sapphires*
shift the emphasis away from the figure. City Art Museum, Birmingham.

effect and treatment are so far apart" (quoted in Denys Sutton, *Nocturne: the Art of James McNeill Whistler*). After 1870, Whistler's art moved away from Moore's, but the two remained on good terms. Moore was the only artist to testify on Whistler's behalf in his libel action against Ruskin, and Whistler dedicated his ensuing publication, *Whistler v. Ruskin: Art and Art Criticism,* to Moore. At Moore's death in 1893, Whistler proclaimed him "the greatest artist that, in the century, England might have cared for and called her own."

What Moore and Whistler both were attempting to do in the late 1860s can be seen in one light as turning away from the naturalism of the Pre-Raphaelites, from the realism of Courbet and from early Impressionism, away from progress, and returning to the academically fostered Neo-Classical fold. The most cogent statement of Whistler's new interests comes in another letter to Fantin-Latour, which John Rewald quotes (in *The History of Impressionism*) as evidence of Whistler's virtual suicide as an artist once he had left the wholesome air of France. In this letter, Whistler bitterly denounced and denied the "disgusting" influence of Courbet: "Ah if only I had been a pupil of Ingres. I don't say that out of any rhapsodical enthusiasm for his pictures; I like them half-heartedly, I found many of the pictures, which we saw together, of a very questionable style, not at all Greek, as is maintained, but very viciously French. I feel that one has much further to go and much more beautiful things to paint. But I repeat—if only I had been his pupil; what a master he would have proved, and how he would have healthily led us" (*Nocturne*).

This is severe reaction indeed: not only are Courbet and his whole influence damned, but even Ingres proves inade-

quate. What Whistler wanted was not to return to French Neo-Classicism, but, on the basis of that, to push on to something fundamentally new and essentially Greek. For Whistler and Moore this was a formalist revolution. Their attempt to be Greek did not mean painting Greek subjects; despite the draperies, not one of their pictures has a subject drawn from ancient history, literature or mythology, and with one exception (a nude by Moore titled *A Venus*) their titles hint at no connection with the classical tradition whatsoever. Someone reading a list of Moore's pictures might assume that he was a painter of rarefied still-lifes, since most of them bear the name of some inconspicuous accessory. These cryptically titled paintings commence with *Pomegranates* and *Apricots,* which Moore exhibited in 1866, and which are compositions of three and two figures respectively. In following years, he exhibited *Azaleas, A Garden, Shells, Pansies, Beads, Garnets, A Workbasket, Yellow Marguerites, White Hydrangeas,* etc., etc., all of which are figural, and in many of which the observer would be hard put to find the objects for which they are named. Moore's titles demonstrate how little the subject of a picture in the conventional sense meant to him. They correspond to the musical titles of Whistler, which first appeared in 1867, and they must have seemed equally inscrutable to the Victorian public.

A reflection of this redirection of interests can be seen in Swinburne's critique of the 1868 Royal Academy. Two pictures impressed him. One was G. F. Watts's *Wife of Pygmalion,* which Swinburne praised "for depth and nobility of feeling and meaning." The other was *Azaleas* by the 27-year-old Moore: "His painting is to artists what the verse of Théophile Gautier is to poets; the faultless and secure expression of an exclusive worship of things formally beauti-

Crucial to Whistler's development was his close friendship with Moore in the late '60s: inspired by the Parthenon frieze, Moore's *Musician,* ca. 1866 (Isaacson collection, New York), is echoed in the composition of Whistler's *Symphony in White, No. 4,* 1868-69 (Tate Gallery, London).

Moore was influenced by Whistler's researches in Japanese design: Whistler's *Mrs. Leyland* [left], 1872-73 (77 inches high; The Frick Collection, New York) and Moore's *The End of the Story,* ca. 1876 (Coats Gallery, New York).

ful. That contents them; they leave to others the labours and the joys of thought or passion. The outlines of their work are pure, decisive, distinct; its colour is of the full sunlight. This picture of *Azaleas* is as good a type as needs be of their manner of work. A woman delicately draped, but showing well the gentle mould of her fine limbs through the thin soft raiment; pale small leaves and bright white blossoms about her and above, a few rose-red petals fallen on the pale marble and faint-coloured woven mat before her feet; a strange and splendid vessel, inlaid with designs of Eastern colour; another—clasped by one long slender hand and filled from it with flowers—of soft white, touched here and there into blossom of blue; this is enough. The melody of colour, the symphony of form is complete: one more beautiful thing is achieved, one more delight is born into the world; and its meaning is beauty; and its reason for being is to be."

To a public instructed by Ruskin to find serious messages in works of art, this must have seemed like airy-fairy nonsense. If not thought and passion, what should art be all about? The answer, of course, is Beauty, "beauty pure and simple," and to the exclusion of all else.

This approach is mainly concerned with what painting is not. However, its negativism coincides with contemporary views of the Greek ideal. Walter Pater devoted a large part of his essay on Winckelmann, which he published in 1867, to a discussion of Greek art in which he praised the happy limits of Greek thought and Greek art: the mind not yet independent of the flesh. The concern of Greek sculpture is pure form; it does not express thoughts. The *Venus of Melos:* "is in no sense a symbol, a suggestion, of anything beyond its own victorious fairness. The mind begins and ends with the finite image, yet loses no part of the spiritual motive. That motive is not lightly and loosely attached to the sensuous form, as its meaning to an allegory, but saturates and is identical with it. The Greek mind had advanced to a particular stage of self-reflexion, but was careful not to pass beyond it."

The limitations of Moore's art, likewise, accompanied

what appear to have been distinct limitations of mind. He lived as a recluse, and his lack of social graces was notorious. Rossetti met him once, found him "a dull dog," and studiously avoided him. Rossetti did not like Moore's art either, "great merits with a good deal of silly conceit and woeful shortcoming," but then Rossetti, who in his later pictures always tried to pack in more symbolic meaning than the subject or his talent would bear, was unlikely to applaud Moore's self-imposed limitations.

Beauty, however, needs more nourishment than just the elimination of thought and passion. Moore's *Musician* borrows from the Greeks not only impassivity of mood. The style of draperies and the pose of the two girls are based on the pediment figures from the Parthenon. There is also a hint of Japan in the spray of leaves projecting into the picture from the right and the three fans cut off along the top. These elements are organized in a shallow space, in which the background wall, running parallel to the picture surface, is so close that the composition has the effect of bas-relief. The paneled dado imposes a two-dimensional geometrical order, which is emphasized by the fans above. In other pictures by Moore the geometrical articulation is extended by a pattern of tiles or a rug on the floor.

Whistler's *Symphony in White, No. 4* shows the same compositional elements with a little less emphasis on the Greek and a little more on the Japanese. This difference accords with what each artist brought with him. When Nesfield arbitrated between Whistler and Moore, he defined their respective contributions: "You [Whistler] have seen and felt Moore's specialité in his female figures' method of clothing and use of coloured muslin; also his hard study of Greek work. Then Moore has thoroughly appreciated and felt your mastery of painting in a light key." Moore's light colors were generally considered Japanese; the *Art Journal* described them as inclining "to tender and tertiary harmonies made known in this country by the large importation of Japanese screens." In this as in the more obvious Orientalisms he followed Whistler's lead. The fans, for example, come from Whistler's *Princesse du Pays de la Porcelaine* in the Freer Gallery.

Whistler's pictures in this vein generally did not reach completion, and after 1869 or 1870 he abandoned them entirely. Apparently he realized that he had neither the technical equipment nor the temperament to paint ambitious figural compositions. His chief works of the 1870s are portraits and the *Nocturnes* which were to cause such a fuss at the Grosvenor Gallery. The latter have little to do with Whistler's classicizing phase, but in the portraits there are

frequent reflections of the interests he shared with Moore. An example is the geometrically patterned floor and dado of *Mrs. Leyland* in The Frick Collection, New York. A slighter point in common between the two artists, which Whistler kept for the rest of his life, is the butterfly monogram he used as a signature. This device, which Whistler began to use in the late 1860s (the *Symphony in White, No. 3*, 1867, is still conventionally signed), echoes the anthemion always used by Moore (it appears to the left of the man's head in *The Musician*).

Moore, in the 1870s, ploughed ever more deeply the same furrow. His most characteristic works are single draped female figures, posed before a cloth backdrop. There is no subject, the women in themselves are boring, and formal composition takes place only within strict limits. The three works illustrated on these pages were all exhibited at the Grosvenor Gallery in 1877 and 1878 and have much in common. The same accessories appear and reappear. Even the pose is repeated. What is left, however, pattern, texture and color, is constantly changing. The colors of *The End of the Story* are basically green and white, of *Sapphires* blue and

An early statement of a great Pre-Raphaelite theme—music—in a medieval setting: Rossetti's *A Christmas Carol*, ca. 1858, watercolor (13½ inches high). Fogg Museum, Cambridge, Mass.

Meticulous realism as a setting for a medieval romance: Burne-Jones *The Beguiling of Merlin*, exhibited at the Grosvenor Gallery in 1877 (72 inches high). Lady Lever Collection, Port Sunlight, Cheshire, England.

orange, of *Birds* lemon yellow, orange and white. Color, which has lost any suggestion of antique austerity, has become the main concern of these pictures, which in purpose are essentially abstract rather than representational. The repetitively posed women are comparable to the squares of Josef Albers or the recurrent shapes of Mark Rothko: a constant theme upon which Moore imposes ever more inventively varied patterns of color.

The theoretical underpinnings of this art are provided by Pater, who in "The School of Giorgione," published ten years after the essay on Winckelmann, attempted to define the role of painting: "In its primary aspect, a great picture has no more definite message for us than an accidental play of sunlight and shadow for a few moments on the wall or floor: is itself, in truth, a space of such fallen light, caught as the colours are in an Eastern carpet, but refined upon, and dealt with more subtly and exquisitely than by nature itself."

Perhaps more than any other nineteenth-century painter, Moore held himself to this decorative ideal; the pictures even look like Eastern carpets. There is no record of any connection between the two men, but before Pater's theories appeared in print, Moore was providing their visual equivalent.

In the same essay Pater made the often-quoted statement, "All art constantly aspires towards the condition of music." By this condition he meant the obliteration of any distinction between matter and form. The form, the mode of handling, should become an end in itself. Among Pater's contemporaries, Whistler and Moore were the only English artists likely to consider this a legitimate goal. For both of them the musical analogy was important. Whistler's musical titles make his purpose insistently clear. In 1868, Swinburne described Moore's *Azaleas* as a "melody of colour," a "symphony of form," and in the same review he returned to musical allusion to describe Whistler's *Six Projects*. In the following year, Moore exhibited a strange picture of togaed musicians, performing anachronistically on violins and cellos, which he titled *A Quartet: A Painter's Tribute to the Art of Music, A.D. 1868.* Music-making was also a frequent subject for many of their esthetic contemporaries, for example, Burne-Jones, whose *Laus Veneris* shows an all-girl band singing the praises of Venus, and, especially, Rossetti, who painted a group of watercolors in 1857 and 1858 which a Pre-Raphaelite colleague suggested were intended to symbolize the association of color and music.

Whether or not Rossetti actually intended such a program, this small group of watercolors is of immense importance for later Victorian painting. Pre-Raphaelite moral earnestness and detailed naturalism have given way to poetic fancy. The embellishments are lavishly medieval, but the subjects are entirely the products of Rossetti's imagination. There is no story and no message other than decorative brightness and the charm of a fairy-tale Middle Ages in which the hours are whiled away with music. Rossetti unfortunately did not

long sustain this mood, and after 1860, his art declined visibly, but his combination of the associative and decorative was the point of departure for the Aesthetic movement. Whistler fell under his spell before coming into contact with Moore; Burne-Jones's career virtually stems from these watercolors; Morris and Swinburne both wrote poetry based upon them.

Although always reminiscent of Rossetti, Burne-Jones's painting is much more varied, and occasionally, as in the tall figure of Nimué and floral background of *The Beguiling of Merlin,* it comes close to Moore's. That Burne-Jones's figure is medieval, while Moore's women remain vaguely antique, does not make much difference; the archeological concern of either artist is about nil. What does matter is that Burne-Jones is illustrating a story, and his success lies in the degree to which he makes us feel that strange and magical things are happening. Likewise, *Laus Veneris* combines decorative richness with a wealth of literary illusion: Swinburne, *Tannhäuser, Under the Hill* and, for us, Mario Praz. Both of these pictures illustrate the fatal woman, although in *Laus Veneris* the blood-stained sensuality of Swinburne's poem has given way to the world-weary lassitude so characteristic not only of Burne-Jones but of later Victorian painting in general.

In Moore's later pictures almost everybody has fallen asleep. Around 1880 he started to paint compositions of several figures which bring the decorative richness of his art to a peak. However, in these paintings, as the impassivity of the 1870s yields to a mood of drowsy indolence, we can sense the dilution of Moore's art. Not surprisingly, these pictures were more influential than his more purely visual painting of the previous decade. The germ for this contagious sleepiness may have come from Rossetti and Burne-Jones, but Moore provided the models for legions of nymphs, muses and allegorical figures who slumber gracefully into the twentieth century. Lord Leighton's *Flaming June* is a spectacular and famous example. In this late work by the President of the Royal Academy, the connection with Moore is obvious; yet we can see how Moore's concerns have been transformed by the addition of background space, by the voluptuousness of the figure and by Leighton's sheer virtuosity. *Flaming June* is accomplished in a way Moore never was, but also in a way he never wanted to be.

We tend to associate the classical tradition in nineteenth-century painting with academicism, but the classicism of Moore and Whistler has little to do with the Academy. Neither was a member of the Royal Academy, nor were Rossetti and Burne-Jones (Burne-Jones was elected an associate member in 1885; he exhibited there once, decided he did not like it and eventually resigned without ever becoming a full member). Aestheticism in England was as much an *avant-garde* movement in terms of what was going on around it as Impressionism in France, however incredibly different the results. Whistler's and Moore's Greek ambitions of the 1860s

In Moore's later pictures almost everybody has fallen asleep:
The Dreamers, ca. 1880 (27 inches high). City Art Museum, Birmingham.

Burne-Jones adapts the theme of sleep to a whole series on the Sleeping Beauty:
The King and His Court, ca. 1872 (24 inches high). Museo de Arte, Ponce, Puerto Rico.

have also been linked with a widespread resurgence of classicism comprising not only Leighton but also such Continental artists as Puvis de Chavannes and Anselm Feuerbach. However, what these artists have in common is chiefly the negative quality of looking to the classical world as a reaction against the prevailing naturalism of their own century. The absence of classical subjects, of nostalgia for a Greek or Roman Golden Age, and of any concern for archeological exactitude separates Whistler and Moore from their classicizing contemporaries. For us, it is perhaps easiest to admire them for this, for what they did not do, to praise them for turning their backs on almost everything that interested their colleagues, and, perhaps, the theory is more accessible to us than the pictures themselves. But their attempt to reduce a work of art to its essentials, in an environment that lavished its attention on inessentials, prefigures concerns of today. In the light of our own changing ideas of what a work of art should be, we shall someday be able to see that the byways of nineteenth-century art reflect the richness of that century's varied interests, and that they often have as much relevance for us as the well-known works of the few artists we hail as its masters.

W BOVGVEREAV 1873

VIII

Antidisestablishmentarianism

By Thérèse Burollet

Thérèse Burollet is curator of the Musée Cognacq-Jay in Paris,
which houses an important collection of Rococo art and furniture.
Long an admirer of the secret qualities of official art of the
1890s, she is completing a work on the cemetery of Père Lachaise.

Systematically thrown on the rubbish-heap of history after
having been alternately vilified and lyrically defended during the Third Republic, all "official" French painting of 1880
to 1914 is now lumped under the vague heading of Academism, i.e., Bad. Furthermore, the celebrated *Indépendants,*
who were the founders of modern art, have incited us to dis-
parage everyone who rejected them. They have ridiculed not
only *pompier* art but also the *Style Nouille* of 1900, which
set out to be different both in form and spirit. This version
of Art Nouveau has recently reawakened a sudden interest
that cannot be explained by publicity alone. Its graphic refinement charms us, accustomed as we are to purely plastic
relationships; and its bizarre, ambiguous climate evokes the
strangeness of seventeenth-century Mannerism and of Surrealism. The same troubled enchantment sends us back to
Mucha and to Pontormo.

On the other hand, the lack of understanding is still total
in regard to the art of the official Salons,[1] all of which is
buried indiscriminately under the academic label.

The term Academism as applied to every non-vanguard
work in the first four decades of the Third Republic could
perhaps be given a purely historical significance which
would no longer sound like a reproach, like the terms Mannerism and Baroque. But is it possible to divide nineteenth-
century painting by separating official art from its great forerunners: J.-L. David, Ingres, Delacroix and their disciples
Flandrin, Delaroche and Couture, who, little by little, are
coming back into their own? As long as the term Academic
keeps its stylistic meaning—that is, the stereotyped repetition
of the art forms of the past, the double imitation of antique
models and consecrated masters—this definition cannot be
uniformly applied to all the artists who were famous and
honored between 1880 and 1914. Today they are condemned
for their technique, their esthetics and their choice of subjects. Yet most of the Salon pictures depicted merely traditional subjects: history, allegory, nudes, genre scenes, neither
more nor less naughty than in the past, portraits, and so on.
Certain themes were, of course, undeniably ridiculous: the
love of a mermaid for a deep-sea diver (Albert Guillaume's
Amour Profond, in the Salon des Artistes Français of 1909)
is hard to defend. But who ever points out Marie's self-satis-
fied air of a matron in her Sunday best in Rubens' *Meeting
of Henri IV and Marie de' Medici,* or Thetis' lascivious position with Jupiter in Ingres' *Jupiter and Thetis?* "Great" art
is universally recognized as a sound value. Yet, though some
pictures were merely mediocre plagiarisms of Flemish in-
teriors or heady anecdotes of the eighteenth century, painting continued in the Third Republic as in previous centuries
to tell a story. This role is no longer necessary: our need for
images and evocation is sated by photography, the cinema
and television. Since Cecil B. de Mille the historical reverie
has been materialized at the level of the masses and vast
murals are no longer required. Lenepveu's *History of Joan
of Arc* in the Pantheon has been surpassed by Victor Flem-

William Bouguereau's name is synonymous with "official" painting.
His *Nymphs and Satyr,* 1873 (101 ¾ inches high) carries academic
eroticism to a culminating frenzy. Clark Institute, Williamstown.

ing's *Joan of Arc,* Rochegrosse's *Death of Caesar* by Mankiewicz's *Cleopatra,* Cormon's *Flight of Cain* by Huston's *The Bible.* The camera has become the recorder of current events. Likewise the image of the female nude has become everyday, almost tangible, and Bouguereau no longer titillates. With the twentieth century, photography triumphs, replacing, among other things, the portrait in its function as a likeness. Modern art can reject the exact reproduction of things, but this hardly justifies rejecting the realism sought by an era which did not have our technical means.

The mass of artists who showed in the Salons produced a fragmentation of styles, an enormous variety of genres, a multiplicity of manners. This "explosion," the expression of the vitality of a society, is a characteristic of turn-of-the-century art which cannot be ignored.

Can the study of academic techniques make our judgment of official painting even more severe? Certainly thousands of canvases of no merit whatever, exhibited in the Salons by unknown artists, should remain in oblivion; and scores of unimportant works by minor masters of no great quality will never be anything but feeble witnesses of their time. But what of famous artists like Cabanel, Jean-Paul Laurens and

Like the other paintings reproduced on these two pages, Joseph Blanc's *Vow of Clovis* was commissioned for the Pantheon in Paris.

The patron saint of Paris was a popular academic subject: Jean-Paul Laurens' *Burial of St. Geneviève,* 1882.

Bouguereau, members of the Institut and honored professors of the Ecole des Beaux-Arts? [2] They could, like all artists, produce failures (such as Bonnat's *Martyrdom of St. Denis* in the Pantheon), but usually their craftsmanship was sure. Their drawings and sketches testify to the skill of their pencil and the passionate spirit of their brush. It is true that they disciplined these gifts, often to the point of aridity, in an attempt to realize works wherein all the component elements—drawing, values, color—were pushed to a maximum intensity. This lack of selectivity disconcerts us, dampens the spirit, creates a feeling almost of embarrassment. Yet it is

rarely the result of impotence, but rather of ambition—an urge toward too much ability and cleverness. Often, nonetheless, the freedom of composition, the arrangement of masses and the sense of the wall to be decorated correct the excesses of studied refinement, and we may find, even in the Pantheon [3] or the Capitol at Toulouse, extremely handsome works painted with a firm brush by Jean-Paul Laurens or Benjamin Constant. Drawing inspiration from the past, from classical compositions, from Spanish or Rubensian color, the official painters nevertheless adapted the ideas of the past to their own sensibilities, sometimes combining sev-

Cabanel's *Life of St. Louis*, another lesson in history, sets up a rhythm of calm vertical lines against the plane of the rear wall.

Jules-Eugène Lenepveu's *Vision of Joan of Arc*, 1889, recalls Gide's statement: "The best intentions make the worst works of art."

eral influences. But so-called academic craftsmanship is not always merely the applied transformation of the lessons absorbed in the studios of the Ecole des Beaux-Arts. The artists also looked around them and assimilated contemporary discoveries, sometimes producing hybrid works, but also opening multiple and differentiated paths of research. Can one in fact reasonably apply the term Academism to Joseph Avy or Albert Besnard, both influenced by Impressionism; to Charles Cottet and Luc Simon, attracted by the dark planes

of the Nabis; or to Henri Martin, seduced by Pointillism? Or even to Elie Delaunay and Ernest Hébert, who are so close to the Pre-Raphaelites?

Its traditional, even outmoded subjects and varied, generally acceptable techniques do not alone explain the uniform ostracism which is the fate in our time of official painting of the 1880s, and even less the similar condemnation which lies over a whole segment of the literature of that time, from René Bazin to Marcel Prévost. The reasons for

Portrait of a Lady by Charles Giron. Petit Palais, Paris.

Countess Castiglione by J.-E. Blanche. Musée Carnavalet.

Philippe Parrot: *Portrait of Sarah Bernhardt,* 1875. Versailles museum.

Edouard Debat-Ponson: *La Maladetta.* Opera, Paris.

Ernest Duez: *The Promenade,* 1873. Arras museum.

Emile Lévy: *Portrait of Barbey d'Aurevilly,* 1881. Versailles museum.

Carolus-Duran's *Portrait of Mlle. de Lancey* deftly plagiarizes Goya's *Maja.* Petit Palais, Paris.

Flag Day, 1880, by Edouard Detaille, anticipates the television screen. Musée Carnavalet, Paris.

The academic sculptor dreams of glory: Albert Maignan's *Carpeaux*, 1892. Amiens museum.

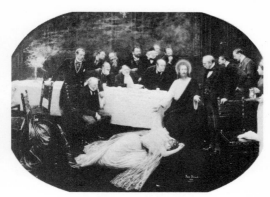

Jean Béraud's *Mary Magdalen in the House of the Pharisee*, 1891, satirizes political figures of the day.

The artist as political reporter: *Session at the Hôtel de Ville* by Henri Coeylas. Musée Carnavalet.

The Official Salon celebrated by one of its illustrious sons: Henri Gervex's *The Jury for Painting*, 1885. Rheims museum.

this rejection are doubtless more profound than mere taste: there is an inward revolt, an unavowed hostility toward everything that went to make up the social atmosphere of the Third Republic before 1914. An order established on the systematic exaltation of moral values and on money repels us. We are irritated by jingoistic patriotism, capitalistic paternalism and mawkish, unconscious or hypocritical sentimentality that delights in popular imagery and tearful melodrama. Furthermore our eroticism makes fun of false modesty, lowered eyelids and unlaced corsets.

Yet even though this period is that of our grandparents' dining-rooms, we ought to have enough perspective to comprehend the sincere aspiration of that society toward its ideals of patriotism, civic and moral stability, social and scientific progress. They were the forces behind a regime that initiated numerous reforms and fought heroically in the first World War.

But we have put everything in question. Patriotism, citizenship, work, religion no longer "pay." We are in the same critical position as the Renaissance toward a world it scornfully called "Gothic" because it no longer understood it. This prevents us from judging fairly the artistic manifestations which are the reflection of the *Belle Epoque*. Just as we now appreciate only plastic innovations, shock, the new, the expression of a freedom that wants to be boundless; so we abhor social realism and displays of manual skill, such as are to be found in the great historical commissions in the Pantheon, the Sorbonne or the Hotel de Ville in Paris, which teach national history. And we abhor them even when they possess

the pictorial qualities necessary and sufficient to make them esteemed.

This is our error. We let murals deteriorate, we destroy pictures, we hide statues and commemorative monuments. Important paintings gather dust in the basements of our museums, where the general public, which is less severe and less unjust, cannot re-evaluate them. This condemnation without appeal seems a proof of a definite lack of catholicism in our understanding of a period which will soon be a century old.

[1] The organization of the official Salon, sponsored by the State since 1673, was entrusted in 1881 to the new Société des Artistes Français. It was held at the Palais de l'Industrie in the Champs-Elysées until 1897, then at the Galerie des Machines and, after 1900, at the Grand Palais. Meissonier split it in two in 1890 to found the Société de la Nationale des Beaux-Arts, in an attempt to escape the tyranny of the jury and to promote different doctrines. Seen from afar, the latter seem very similar to their predecessors. The Nationale was held in the Champ de Mars.

[2] The great *pompier* masters were all-powerful and no one could succeed without their support: members of the Académie des Beaux-Arts, they chose the Prix de Rome winners. They usually taught at the Ecole des Beaux-Arts. They also dominated the jury of the Société des Artistes Français, where they distributed various prizes.

[3] The Pantheon is the paradise of French official art in Paris. It houses historical paintings by the principal masters: Jean-Paul Laurens, Cabanel, Galland, Bonnat, Detaille, Puvis de Chavannes, Lenepveu, Humbert, etc., as well as sculptures by Bartholomé, Marqueste and Sicard. The Salle des Illustres in the Capitol at Toulouse is a veritable museum of academic art; notable are *The Wall* by Jean-Paul Laurens (1897) and *The Entry of Urban II* by Benjamin Constant.

Fastidious archeological reconstruction: Jean Lecomte du Noüy's *The Bearers of Bad Tidings*. Tunis museum.

In Tony Robert-Fleury's *Last Days of Corinth*, 1870, the central group of women recalls Delacroix. Louvre.

The Shereef's Justice by Benjamin Constant prefigures the cinematic orgies of Erich von Stroheim. Lunéville museum.

From Hugo's *Légende des Siècles:* J.-A. Leroux's *Confidence of Marquis Fabrice*. Hugo museum, Paris.

Modesty: Jules Lefebvre's *Lady Godiva*. 1890. Amiens museum.

Heroism: Jean-Joseph Weerts' *The Death of Joseph Bara*.

Ecstasy: Jacques-Clément Wagrez' *The Ecstasy of St. Clare*, 1884.

Sketch for *The Stone Age*, 1882, by Fernand Cormon, a specialist in prehistoric genre. Carcassonne museum.

Gustave Courtois: *The Funeral of Atala*, 1894, illustrating Chateaubriand's romantic tale.

Pointillist experiment: Ferdinand Humbert's *Charity*. Pantheon, Paris.

A striking evocation of Caravaggio: Henry Lerolle's *Arrival of the Shepherds*. Carcassonne museum.

An ever-popular theme: *Joan of Arc*, 1896, by George William Joy, an Englishman working in Paris. Rouen museum.

Meticulous realism and suave composition: Etienne Gautier's *St. Cecelia*. Cathédrale Saint-Jean, Lyon.

Jules Rougeron: *A Carmelite Taking the Veil*, 1889. Dijon museum. "Art consists in exact and total imitation"—Taine.

Uneasy mélange of realism and mystic symbolism: *Christ Walking on the Water*, 1891, by Ernest Duez.

Gérome working from life: *Recreation in a Russian Camp*, 1858—conscript
soldiers enjoying themselves under the supervision of a guard with a knout.

details are never automatic, but always freshly observed,
especially in terms of light and color, and they are painted
with a care that shows a fanatical love for paint and painting.

Although he sticks to the quieter moments of life, his
range of subjects is wide. He borrowed heavily from the
repertory of Dutch genre themes which Daumier had revi-
talized earlier in the century. In antiquity he imagined, and
in North Africa he observed, the same pastimes which the
Dutch masters and Daumier saw around themselves at home:
parties and brawls in inns, musicians and their rapt audi-
ences, children's games, chess players, silent smokers, people
at prayer.

Some of the incidents in his genre works are rather involved, and take careful reading. He remedies what could
be a tendency towards the trivial by the intimacy of his nar-
ration; he makes us step up close to the canvas to notice the
nuances that lead enjoyably through the picture.

And, of course, his technique is astounding. No one has
ever denied that. It is sure, prodigious, never faltering in
control or interest. The room and atmosphere built for the
characters of *The Grey Eminence* are a triumph of imagination and skill. The sense of humor in the figure of the incorruptible monk is suggested throughout the picture: in the
clothing and gestures of the obsequious but uneasy courtiers, in the sagging tapestry on the stairwell. The figures
are grouped with a skill that only Degas among his contem-

poraries could rival, and they move with a personal sover-
eignty over balance and gesture. They are not so graceful as
Degas might have drawn them, but Gérome is more of a
realist than Degas.

His color is luscious, "luminous and alluring," and freshly
invented for each picture, according to the mood. Intense,
resonant darks contrast with bright warm colors whose
highlights never betray white lead near the surface. In an
old-fashioned but sure way he builds his color schemes up
from the tint of the ground and pushes his color range to
extremes in both directions. The final glaze is a mixture of
small varied strokes that paint the patterns of light. When
a work fails, it is usually because the main tone was an
unhappy choice, but this happens to him less often than to
Renoir. Indeed, it is more often his drawing that flags—from
indifference or old age—than his color.

Gérome started his public career at the same time as Courbet, in the salons of the late 1840s. They both came to maturity during the heyday of Realism, and each championed a
different kind of Realism. Gérome had studied with Delaroche, that careful constructor of theatrical historical scenes
(such as *The Little Princes in the Tower*) and with Gleyre,
who taught whole generations of painters (including Renoir
and Monet) how to pose and paint nudes. In 1844 Gérome
accompanied Delaroche to Rome. There he studied, assisted
his master, built up a repertory of Italian subjects and became, at the same time, an enthusiastic and learned amateur

103

Reporter's eye in North Africa: *Soldiers Playing Checkers*, 1896 (7⅜ inches high), chalk. Clark Institute, Williamstown, Mass.

Inscribed *To My Daughter Madeleine*, this Middle-East genre painting bears a disquieting compositional similarity to Gérome's reconstruction of Rembrandt's studio [p. 105, top]. R.I. School of Design Museum, Providence.

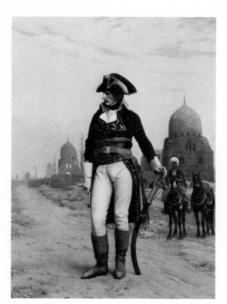

Napoleon in Cairo, ca. 1885 (14 inches high), an example of Gérome's occasional return to historical themes within the context of Arab genre that mostly occupied him after the mid-1870s. Princeton Museum.

Gérome: The Academic Realist

archeologist. His master had developed in him a good eye for the costumes, furniture and decor of other eras, and Gérome—inspired by Ingres—gave his attention to the artifacts of antiquity. It was inevitable that he would be drawn to the antique manner of Ingres, for he already imitated him in his first portraits and in his drawings. He started to paint small erotic genre scenes in Neo-Classical settings.

In 1847 one of these works was shown in the salon, the famous *Cock Fight* (now in a store-room of the Louvre; if it were displayed, it would be the only Gérome on view in a public collection in Paris). The figures are almost life-size, the work is impeccably if dryly painted. The most interesting element, after the austerity of the composition, is the subject matter, for, despite its size, it is a genre work. The scene could have been translated from Brouwer or Steen. Two years later Courbet was to make his mark at the Salon with another oversize genre work, *After Dinner at Ornans*. With men sitting around a table smoking and making music, it, too, could be called an amplified Brouwer, if not a classicized one.

Despite the earthiness of its subject matter, *The Cock Fight* caught the attention of that famous esthete, Théophile Gautier, who probably thought he saw in Gérome's precious primitive style the possibilities of a counter-movement to the more earth-bound Realism of the day. He described and praised the picture at such length in his review of the Salon in *L'Artiste* that Gérome was at once made famous. A small group of artists formed around him, mostly from Gleyre's studio, all painting precious, erotic genre scenes in antique settings. The style was a reaction against the lofty themes of traditional history painting, not a continuation of the practice. The group called itself the *Néo-grecs* or the *Pompeïstes*. Gérome painted some of his best pictures in this style, elegantly balanced in glowing colors, full of intimate details, and almost always small in format, like the lovely *Socrates Seeking Alcibiades in the House of Aspasia*, which demands our attention (as well as a bit of erudition) to enjoy.

Gérome had ambitions of becoming something more important than a painter of Greek and Roman genre. He planned a large historical allegory for the Salon, *The Age of Augustus, the Birth of Christ*. The composition—based on Ingres' *Apotheosis of Homer*—was to show members of the conquered nations of the Empire at the feet of Augustus, throned before the Temple of Mars. In the hope of finding ethnic models for the subjugated tribesmen, Gérome headed with a companion for the steppes of Russia. On the way they became entranced by the Danube basin and followed it downstream to the domains of the Russians and the Turks.

His gigantic composition, *The Age of Augustus*, was shown at the Salon of 1858. It is now in the Picardy museum, Amiens, where its size defies photography and display: it is about 21 by 30 feet and is kept rolled up in the basement. Along with this allegory he hung at the salon a very small picture—almost as an afterthought, for it is not in the catalogue—a genre scene from his trip, *A Study from Life, Recreation in a Russian Camp*. The Russian occupa-

Gérome's repertory of subjects included art history: *Rembrandt Etching,* in the 1861 Salon.

Twilight Procession at the Court at Versailles (32½ inches high), in the Salon of 1896, produced a controversy over the rising moon, which Gérome removed and then afterwards reinstated.

Death of Caesar, 1865 (33⅝ inches high), detailed historical reconstruction predicting Cinemascope. Walters Gallery, Baltimore.

Dancer, ca. 1895 (10¾ inches high), combines marble with bronze, a classical technique revived by Gérome and popularized in Art Nouveau bibelots. Landau-Alan Gallery, N. Y.

Gérome: The Academic Realist

tion armies in the Balkans were mainly composed of forced conscripts who occupied their own countries. Gérome had painted a small group of these men "enjoying" a concert played by their company band, all under guard. The figures are carefully drawn, even to the misfitting uniforms; the ironic quality makes the work touching as well as curious. *The Age of Augustus* received polite and serious reviews, but *The Recreation in a Russian Camp* was acclaimed, and Gérome was welcomed into the camp of the Realists.

Gérome soon became an avid traveler. In 1856 he made his first trip to Egypt. With a group of friends he rented a boat in Cairo, and traveled up the Nile for six months. The party hunted and made many excursions along the way, and of course, Gérome sketched constantly. As a result of the trip, he exhibited in the next Salon several scenes of what we would call Oriental genre, but which were then called "ethnographic paintings." These scenes continued the naturalism of the Russian army scenes, but in more exotic surroundings, and were quite devoid of the mannerisms of the *Néo-grec* works: the many views of soldiers, peasants, dancing girls have a poetry that comes from the subjects themselves, and which resists self-conscious evocation. He saw in Egypt almost the same themes that he had imagined in antiquity: card games, slave auctions and nude concubines.

He painted several splendid Egyptian landscapes, among them *The First Kiss of the Sun.* In it a safari camp is pitched not far from the great pyramids at Giza. It is just before dawn, the camels move restlessly, ropes and tent ends flap in the breeze. Everything is seen with a sharpness of line that reminds one of Caspar David Friedrich, but with a softness of atmosphere that is Gérome's own specialty. The first rays of sunlight touch the tops of the pyramids, causing the stones to glow pink. And by some mysterious touch of his brush, Gérome has caused the vapors of the earth to rise at the base of the pyramids.

For the next few decades he made regular trips to Egypt on safaris which he himself organized. Large groups of friends accompanied him, many of them authors, painters and photographers in search of "Oriental color." Paul Le-

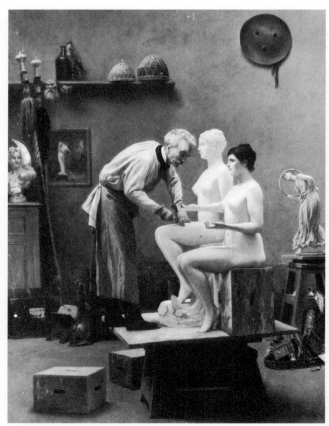

The Artist and His Model, ca. 1877, is Gérome's portrait of himself working faithfully from the motif, surrounded by some favorite props.

In *Pygmalion and Galatea* (35 inches high), a sculpture literally becomes a figure. Metropolitan Museum, N. Y.

noir's *The Fayoum, or Artists in Egypt* (London, 1873) is a direct product of one such safari.

During the 'sixties and 'seventies, while Gérome was most active as a traveler, he showed a surprising number of pictures at the Salon in an even more surprising variety of styles and subjects. For instance, *Alcibiades at the House of Aspasia* was shown in the Salon of 1861 along with *Rembrandt Etching a Plate,* and two Egyptian genre scenes. During the same time he painted contemporary hunt scenes, portraits, landscapes and historical scenes set in antiquity and in eighteenth-century France.

Since Courbet's debut, critics had been declaring that history painting was dead and that artists should limit themselves to things they could see. But traditionally trained painters like Gérome did not want to let history painting die. Despite the popularity of Realism, they dreamed of the multi-figured compositions with heroic themes for which their studies had prepared them. They thought they could satisfy the demand for a feeling of *actuality* with one of *probability*: they would paint history scenes as if they had been there when they occurred. Unfortunately, this very personal sense of the event often reduced it to anecdote.

In *The Death of Caesar,* 1865, Gérome seemed to achieve a balance between history and Realism: the shock of witnessing a murder coincides with the realization that mankind has been betrayed. The props of circumstance are also the props of the betrayal. One reads the treachery and the course of the event in the scrolls on the floor, the overturned throne, the traces of blood. The perspective is arranged so that the viewer feels he is sitting in the same place where the event took place, but still, he sees the corpse through the distance of history.

The skill which Gérome showed in achieving such a solution made him a leader to a slightly younger generation of academic Realists. Several of them worked very closely with him, either as friends or students, including Manet, Degas, Léon Bonnat, the Belgian Alfred Stevens and the American Thomas Eakins. Each one tried personally to save history painting, and each one, individually, deserted it.

Edouard Manet, the most conservative of the lot, resisted Realism as long as he could. His early career is a series of attempts to paint large histories in the old grand manner. After the failure of the *Incident in the Bullring* and the *Execution of Maximilian,* he turned to genre subjects. At the same time Bonnat turned to portraits. Degas persisted longer in painting histories, and then he too went over to painting genre. However, as long as his failing eyesight permitted, Degas used the techniques of history painting in his genre works, as his elaborate perspectives and anatomical studies reveal.

Gérome was older than these painters and more conservative. He held to the notion of history painting just a bit longer. His first reaction was to become a Realist history painter. The preciousness and eroticism of the *Néo-grec*

style, as in *Alcibiades,* gave way to archeological correctness, as in *The Death of Caesar.* The historical scenes gave way to a carefully researched, grandiose genre, as in the famous gladiatorial scenes.

While his classical pictures became archeological, the themes of his Turkish and Egyptian genre developed into elaborate anecdotes, as in the famous *The Prisoner* in the Nantes museum. By the mid 1870s, he had almost ceased painting histories. Landscapes, simple genre scenes, along with a few bullfights and a side-line of lions were his subjects. Occasionally, throughout the rest of his life, he returned to an historical theme, but over two-thirds of his total output seems to be Oriental genre. Many of these canvases are small, careful studies of single figures against exotic backgrounds, usually in the typical costumes of North Africa. An example is the fine *Napoleon at Cairo,* in the Princeton Art Museum.

Late in life he became a sculptor. He worked very faithfully from models, as we can see in the picture he painted of himself at work in his studio. In the name of Realism he tinted or polychromed his statues. In the name of classicism he tried to revive a type of chryselephantine sculpture by combining marble and bronze. It is not generally recognized that he was the inventor of this popular Art Nouveau technique. His active contribution to the movement is seen in the elegant lines of a small bronze nude from his last years.

When he died in his sleep in 1904, a productive life of 60 years ended. He would have gone to his classes at the Ecole the next day, where Fernand Léger was one of his students. Léger praised him, as did all of his students, for not interfering with personal styles, while, at the same time, always knowing how much each student was learning and needed to learn. He taught drawing, which he called "the grammar of painting," and encouraged his students to see with naïve eyes. Naïveté was the basis of his Realism, and he encouraged all of his students to preserve or develop it. One artist who very conscientiously took and followed his advice was the Douanier Henri Rousseau.

Even though he was popular, recognized and rich during his lifetime, Gérome was never a critical success. He had the enthusiastic support of Gautier at the beginning of his career, but other important critics, like Émile Zola, disliked him from the start, and his contribution to each Salon was greeted with bad reviews. Critics still heap abuse upon him, but now without bothering to look at his works. The more famous Academic Realists, his friends Manet and Degas, have been elevated into the ranks of the Impressionists—where they don't comfortably fit at all—and he has been left in oblivion. He is worth rescuing. His works are not only beautiful, they are serious, full of integrity, variety and poetry. And they were so carefully painted that they will survive in good condition until they are brought out into the light again.

Ernest Meissonier: *The Sergeant's Portrait*,
1874. Collection of Baron Schroeder.

Dali comments: "This picture is an illustration of microphysics. The
instantaneity of the glances forms an anti-gravitational structure, like
that which may be suggested in painting by the trajectories of flies or
of pi-mesons. The painter is looking at the sergeant. Three people are
looking at the painter's drawing. One is looking at the dog. The sergeant
and the smoker look at nothing. The whole permits an antiproton explosion.

X

The Incendiary Firemen

By Salvador Dali

A master Surrealist (he once defined painting as the "hand-made photographs of dreams") pays homage to his ancestors, the famous academicians whose extraordinary realism still challenges his own.

Our era has seen the publication of a staggering number of books dealing with contemporary art. Almost none have been devoted to those heroic painters called the *"pompiers."* [1] For a period so utterly dominated by information of all kinds, this is a unique phenomenon. We have a fantastic choice of albums of colorplates on the work of Picasso, Utrillo or Dufy, but you will look in vain for anything on Bouguereau, Meissonier or Detaille. And yet who today can continue to affirm without blushing that Dufy is a more important artist than Meissonier?

The *pompier* painters, especially the glorious Meissonier and Detaille, found in their own time nothing less than the "structure" of the most important subject in the history of civilization: the history of our time itself, at its most complex, dense, tragic, ineluctable, climactic. Detaille in particular discovered in the structure of the most important subject (I repeat: the historical subject) what is most rigorous, hierarchical, physical, biological, nuclear, cellular, atomic; i.e.: *"the infrastructure, the military structure and superstructure, the most explosive of all that exist."* To the point where Detaille, despite all the accepted notions (which are the result of contemporary esthetic myopia), will soon be ranked as the supreme painter of the *living structures* of the future, just as Cézanne will be known as the supreme painter of the *withered structures* of the past.

The great explosion of the sublime period of 1900, still known today as the *Style Nouille* ["noodle style"], was preceded· by the music of Richard Wagner (*Tristan and Isolde,* 1857-59); the philosophy of Friedrich Nietzsche (1844-1900); the genius of Barbizon, François Millet, whose erotic can-

nibalism radiated into "the tragic myth of Millet's *Angelus"* (1858-59), which broods over the *pompiers* Meissonier and Detaille, themselves destined to accomplish the historic mission of perpetuating the genetic code of the fatherland through the flesh and the spirit of Karl Marx (*Das Kapital,* 1867), Max Planck, Friedrich Hegel, Albert Einstein, Sigmund Freud, Antonio Gaudi, Cézanne, Marcel Proust, Raymond Roussel, Mariano Fortuny, Pablo Picasso (b. 1881) and his contemporary Norbert Wiener (1894-1964), who came out of Raymundo Lulio; and the monarchical domes of Buckminster Fuller, which in turn came out of Louis XVI's architect, Ledoux. Since 1900 there has been *nothing, absolutely nothing new:* we have been living on the debris and the rubble of more and more minimal explosions, down to the tiny helpings of the minimal art of today.

Summary list of explosions:

Millet exploded into Seurat and Dali, driving van Gogh mad in passing. Detaille, with his micro-structures, explodes into Cézanne, Cubism and anecdotal Surrealism. Gustave Moreau with his swarming mythology explodes not only through the work of his most notorious students, Matisse and Rouault, but also into the LSD of oneiric and automatic Surrealism. Boldini's whiplash graphism explodes into Mathieu's calligraphy; Gaudi and Fortuny explode into Picasso and Miro; and so on and so forth. Picasso's *Guernica* is a delayed-action explosion of Carolus-Duran's *Murdered Woman.* The *pompier* Cormon is an unexpected prehistoric explosion of Millet and, to top it all, Gérome explodes in the hands of Marcel Duchamp: the optician has a hot seat, the heat of a Minim. Because, in Gala's proverbial phrase, it is always those who are against who are the last ones to understand. Conclusion: Fortuny, the most inspired of all, explodes into Willem de Kooning, who is the most inspired of them all.

Finally, Mr. J.-P. Crespelle in his book *Les Peintres de la Belle Epoque* proves totally and apotheosisistically the utter misunderstanding of *pompier* art that exists intact down to this day. He writes:

"Suppressed during several decades, the taste for Salon painting from before 1914 now reappears, thanks to the excesses, the pirouettes, the absurdities of the avant garde; whether it be *informel,* gestural, miserabilist or neo-Dadaist. Disconcerted, disgusted collectors have by a kind of boomerang reflex turned their attention back to descriptive painting and 'well-made' work, which takes on the supplementary prestige of a period with the nostalgic charm of a paradise lost. To the point where we can no longer really make fun of those artists who often joined love of their profession to a professional conscience that is disdained today. The smile they provoke is tinged with regrets."

Dali says no, no, no! No boomerang! On the contrary: everything in the avant-garde happens necessarily and ineluctably, like the deadly or invigorating debris of the explosion of 1900. After the flushed toilet of microphysics, after Pop, Op and the minimal consequences, we shall see *pompier* art once again very much alive, fresh as a rose and quantified by everything that will have taken place meanwhile in our contemporary esthetic drama, one of the most grandiose and tragic in history.

1 *Pompier*—literally, a fireman. Various origins are given for the adjectival use of this word to describe a style that is "banal and emphatic" (Larousse). One argument supposes that it comes from the resemblance of the neo-Greek helmets favored by members of the Academy in their Neo-Classic battle scenes to the brass helmets of French firemen. Another places it in a remark by Degas about Academic painters: *"C'est les pompiers qui se mettent en feu"* ("The firemen are setting fire to themselves"). —Ed.

Edouard Detaille: *The Dream*, 1888.

Dali remarks: "Chain-structures of the discontinuity (and, for the same price) of the ondulatory and corpuscular light of the pre-scientific dream. *Olé!*"

Detaille: *Saluting the French Wounded.*

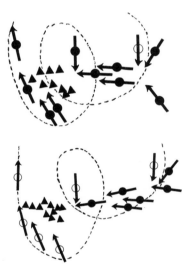

Dali: "At first glance these two paintings of Detaille seem merely to be faithfully transcribed anecdotes, photographs of reality. On an intuition of Mr. Salvador Dali, a study of their structure was undertaken which reveals the following. Suppose that an arrow on a black circle indicates a cavalryman in black, and an arrow on a white circle one in white, and that the black triangles represent the footsoldiers in black. The graphs are practically identical—the same number of arcs and the same trajectories, with the following exceptions. The direction of the black horsemen is inverted within the logarithmic spiral indicated by the arrows. The white horsemen and the footsoldiers remain unchanged. The stationary footsoldiers mark the axis of the spiral."

Detaille: *Saluting the German Wounded.*

Gérome: Optician's sign in rebus form, 1902, [left] and Duchamp's Mona Lisa: *L.H.O.O.Q. Rasé*, 1964. Cordier & Ekstrom, New York.

Dali: "The Oedipal-anal complex in Gérome's work would be evident to any psychoanalyst, as it was to Duchamp."

Boldini: *Portrait of Réjane* [left], and Mathieu: *For Elizabeth of Austria*.

"Boldini's whiplash graphism explodes into Mathieu's calligraphy."

Horace Vernet: *Horace Vernet's Studio*.

Dali points out: "All the elements of a contemporary Happening are here, down to the marijuana smoker [right] with a long pipe for the kif of the period." Identifiable among others are the painters Eugène Lami [left], with trumpet, and Vernet, the duelist in profile.

ABOVE: "Self-explanatory detail" chosen by Dali from Meissonier's *Napoleon III at Solferino* [right], 1863 (17 inches high). Louvre, Paris.

Picasso: *Science and Charity*, 1896-97.
Private collection, Barcelona.

Dali says: "This picture was shown in the autumn of 1966 to 400 brains of polytechnicians in excellent condition, not one of which was able to identify it as a Picasso. Yet no one could deny that it contains all the 'bits' of information in his future work: the watch, the limp hand, the sisters of mercy protecting the progeny. Every July I send a telegram to Picasso, which reads: 'For July, neither women nor snails.' "

"Neither watch, nor woman, nor child, nor snails."

Meissonier: *The Deathbed*, 1838.
Fodor Museum, Amsterdam.

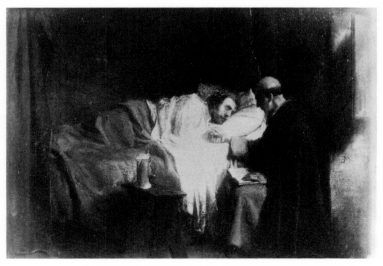

XI

The Academy in Totalitaria

By Harold Rosenberg

Critic, polemicist, poet, Harold Rosenberg is a keen observer
of sociological as well as art trends. His books include
The Tradition of the New, The Anxious Object and *Arshile Gorky.*
He is on the graduate faculty of the University of Chicago.

A distinction needs to be made between academic art based on classical and Renaissance models and the academizing process by which all styles are in time tamed and made to perform in the circus of public taste. Academic art is exemplified by MacMonnies' *Civic Virtue;* the academizing process by the conversion of Pollock's drip paintings into teaching aids for cool canvas-stainers. People who speak of "academic modernism" or the "modern academy," meaning run-of-the-mill Abstract-Expressionism, Pop or Op, confuse the academic convention with art that has become conventional. The true academician will fight like the devil against conventions other than his own no matter how old hat they are. To him the question is, "At what point did art history go off the track?" And his answer up to now has been: "After Impressionism." Picasso to the academician is still a faker, Braque and Mondrian rug designers: they have violated the canons of Beauty and verisimilitude and nothing that has happened, or that can happen, in art or in the history of mankind will ever redeem them.

Compared to the academician, the academic modernist is an esthetic rebel, i.e., one who modulates an authority derived from the past with the superstition of Progress. Modern art is inconceivable without an impatience, at times amounting to disgust, with that vast pile of gilt-framed or marble-pedestaled images of noble and powerful personages, allegorical dramas, glorious landscapes and piazzas known as the Art of the Past—impatience even with the best of it. The task of the modernist academician, whether painter or critic, is to behave as if this impatience never existed, or, if it did, that it is illegitimate. Like the academician, the academic modernist believes in Beauty—the word, as well as the word "inspiration," has lately been reappearing among vanguardist esthetes—and he too cannot tolerate art that has gone off the track. But he swallowed Picasso and Mondrian long ago and is convinced that by a teleological magic Beauty changes to correspond to the kind of art called for by his esthetic timetable.

Between the genuine academician and the academic modernist the former is by far the more serious—his views by their very nature verge on the political, and solicit practical support from conservative social forces (including conservatives who count themselves as progressives and even radicals). The academic modernist merely slows down the pulse of art by functioning as a coagulant of its vital fluids; he represents the natural slackness that overtakes periods of creation. The academician wants to stop certain things from happening in art and he believes that society ought to help him accomplish that aim. He is an embattled idealist, a believer, potentially militant, in a set of values capable of surmounting the "decadence" of the times. His position is fixed; he stands rooted in the sublime, as embodied in rules and procedures abstracted from the masterpieces of all the ages—in his imagination the art of Greece, Egypt, Babylon, the Far East, the Renaissance have been fused into a single substance. The

Hitler in his self-made uniform—part generalissimo, part apocalyptic chauffeur—standing someplace in between Valhalla and Munich: *The Leaders,* by Fritz Erler, 1939.

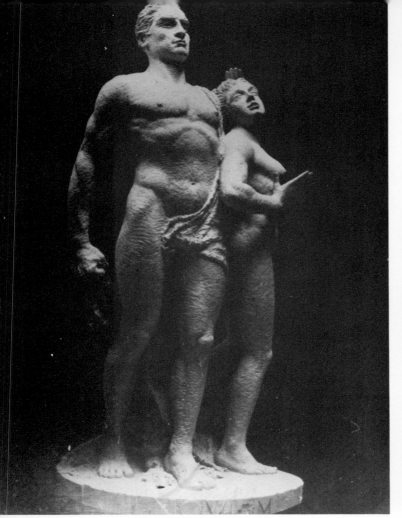

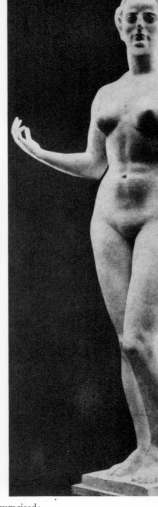

This obscure erotic allegory celebrates
the Italian Fascists' crisis with the League
of Nations: *November 18, 1935*, by Boldrin.

In Nazi sculpture, male nudes are conspicuously uncircumcised:
Wine and *Hospitality*, two of a group of monumental figures for
the official Guest House in Berlin, carved by Josef Thorak, 1939.

academician opposes modern art not out of love for the past (which is after all the present of those who came before), but out of distaste for all periods, except insofar as they appear in forms uplifted by art. It is as the representative of this uplifted sphere that the academician offers his services to the rich and powerful, as well as to the pious masses. His art is a mold in which personages and events may be reshaped into glory. Unlike the academic modernist, who is a mere purveyor of the fashionable, the academician, like the priest, holds the keys to eternal life, to a grandeur above history.

The affinity between the academy and totalitarianism lies in their common wish to transcend the modern world. Both seek to legitimatize themselves through affiliation with noble ancestors. In a cathedral in Braunschweig a few years ago I was shown the tomb of Henry the Lion, a medieval German nobleman whom Heinrich Himmler had elected as his historical alter ego—identifications of this sort meant big commissions for the sculptors and architects of the Third Reich. In this revivalist aspect of totalitarianism the academy is its natural ally, although individual academicians may be morally repelled by the repressive activities of the patron State.

It was during the first modern-style totalitarian regime, that of Napoleon III, described by Karl Marx as a "regime lifted above classes," that academic art, the art lifted above

the real, reached the height of its prestige and blew itself up into an international style. The *luftmensch* Emperor, in whose reign the balloon became a topic of popular interest, was the grand patron of academic painting and sculpture. Napoleon the Little needed to inflate himself with the prestige of Napoleon Bonaparte as Cabanel needed to evoke Titian.

Bonaparte himself had needed to resurrect the noble Romans; even in their revolutionary heyday, Marx pointed out, the bourgeoisie could not play their part in history without dressing up in old costumes. The spirit of the academy thus hovers over the modern state as the expression of the will of its rulers to elevate themselves above the social realities of the time. The refusal of artists since the middle of the nineteenth century to serve as accessories to the transcendental masquerade of bourgeois political, military, industrial and religious powers is at the root of the split of the art of our epoch into academic and modern.

The fact that twentieth-century totalitarian political parties have without exception (though in varying degrees of fanaticism) chosen academic art as their official mode exposes far more decisively than any analysis of their ideological statements the fraudulence of their revolutionary pretentions, their fear of change, and the half-demented impulse of their leaders to perform under the shadow of super-historical doubles. The situation is summed up in the portrait of Hitler by Fritz Erler [see p. 114]. The Führer, standing

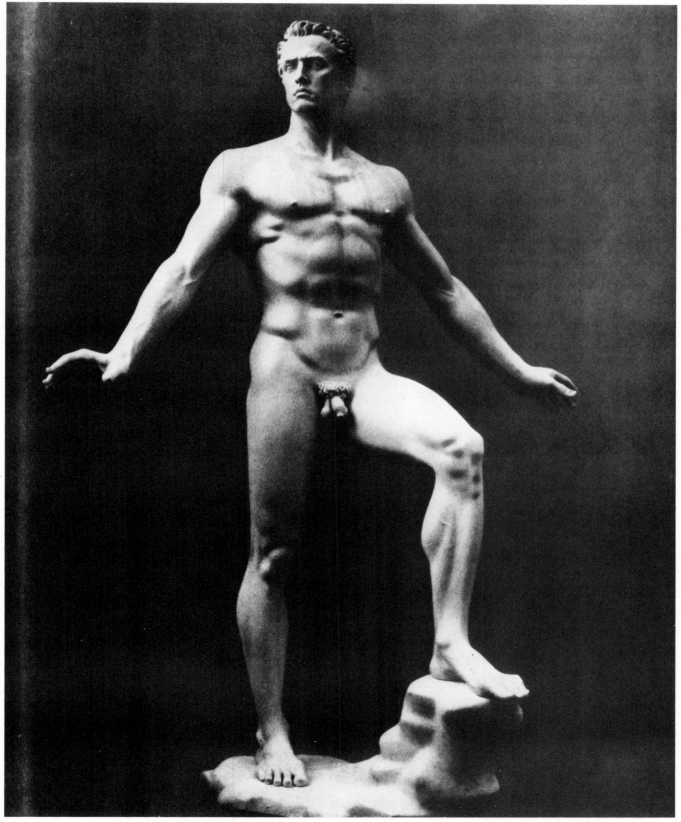

The Victor, 1940, by Arno Breker, the Nazis' favorite sculptor; he took cool eroticism to new heights of obscenity.

on a parapet in no-place, a construction no doubt commemorating the talents of Adolph the Architect, in his concocted uniform with hat and gloves held properly in his hands, could be anything from a marshal of the Wehrmacht to the chauffeur of a fashionable actress. Behind Mr. Anybody, however, looms the mythical hero in stone profile, an eagle on his palm like a bomber on the deck of an aircraft carrier, and with a mace or a fasces in his other brawny fist. "Never," said Hitler in 1937, "was humanity in its appearance and in its feeling closer to classical antiquity than to-day."

A similar conviction about the resemblance of the present to the classical past (a resemblance celebrated in the theory of "Marxist Humanism") had animated the Soviet Union when it drove out or silenced its "Leftists," artists like Kandinsky, Malevich, Tatlin, Rodchenko, and, long before Molotov and von Ribbentrop signed their pact against the democracies, encouraged an art that would blend with that of the Fascists and Nazis. In the U.S.S.R. academicism had to struggle against the conscience of a generation of radical intellectuals who shared Marx's contempt for idealization and hero worship. This handicap was soon liquidated, however, by the megalomania of the party leaders and by the Bolshevik obsession with providing edifying models for the masses. At the outset of the revolution the bulk of the academicians had run off with the Whites; it was only after the defeat of the counter-revolution that many began to filter back. But it was they who represented Art to the Communist leaders, not the radical painters and sculptors who had

ranged themselves on the side of the upheaval (a similar relationship developed in New York in the 'thirties when the Communist-organized Artists and Writers "Congresses" pushed the left-wing painters and poets out of sight in favor of personalities like Rockwell Kent).

There was an element in Lenin's philosophy that closed the door on modernist experimentation in art, and traces of it even in Trotsky. But it was under Stalin that the Academy developed the exclusive power by which Russian art is still strangled. Soviet painting and sculpture, slightly held back from indulging in the ugliest aspects of academic transcendentalism by the Socialist tradition and the Russian folk spirit, were soon loaded with demi-gods manifesting themselves in humble settings—in its sheer bathos Efanov's double portrait of Stalin and Molotov among the daisies needs only an outdoor barbecue and Nixon's dog to be a match for anything in American election-year publicity [see p. 120].

To suppress the actualities of contemporary life, totalitarian academicism transposes them into school-book illustrations. The picture of the hero as educator reappears again and again; it is a motif into which the academic artist as tutor of the ideal can wholeheartedly project himself. Hitler brings the word to representatives of all classes [see p. 119]; Lenin, according to the lying painter backed up by Stalin, exhorts the workers, peasants and soldiers [see p. 119]; and an academic painting in the Tretyakov gallery lectures Red Army men on Art. [see p. below]

A painting superior to the general run of Social Realist illustrations, Gerasimov's *Lenin on the Tribune* [see p. 120]

Official artist depicts proletarians enjoying official art:
G. Gorelov's *Red Army Men in the Tretyakov Gallery, Moscow,* 1938

The official lie sanctified by official art: in *Lenin's Arrival at Petrograd, 1917*, by V. Serov, Stalin is shown conspicuously behind Lenin, although Stalin was not present at all. Serov painted the picture in 1937.

Mythology for a dictator: Hermann O. Hoyer titled this reconstruction of an early Hitler meeting *In the Beginning Was the Word*, after the opening line of the Gospel of St. John.

The banner of victory: *Lenin on the Tribune* by Gerasimov, 1935.

The Academy in Totalitaria

The friendly leaders: *Stalin, Molotov and Children* by Efanov, 1947.

A Chinese version: *The Red Banner* by Chao Yu, 1950 (Sovfoto).

raises the ante by sinking the crowd way down in the distance and directing the hero's address, Prospero-like, toward creatures of the upper air; waves of the Red Banner assume the shape of both sea and ship, which Lenin, mounted above history, rides like Nike, goddess of Victory, already transformed into a figurehead of the Revolution.

Educating the masses and inspiring them to more heroic efforts are the stated purposes of totalitarian art programs, and the pictorial and symbolic idealizations of academic art

The friendly leader: *Chairman Mao among the Masses* by Hou Yi-min, Chou Ling-chao and Teng Shu (Eastfoto).

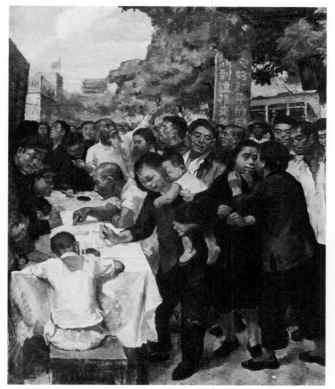

Happy, politically alert workers: *Signing the Stockholm Appeal* ["ban the bomb"] by Tai Chieh, 1950 (Sovfoto).

are, of course, best suited to this end. In the democracies most of the functions of educational and propaganda art have been taken over by commercial studios. But there is one thing that commercial art cannot do, and that is to elevate ruling personages and selected historical events into the lasting realm of Great Art. It is to preserve the immortalizing power of "fine" art that totalitarianism attacks modern styles in painting and sculpture, while often permitting them to flourish in poster design, illustration, caricature and advertis-

ing. Yet it is an error to regard the totalitarian's preference for academic art and his assaults on modernism as based entirely on practical considerations. Russian Futurists and Constructivists could have been extremely useful in Soviet life, and their enthusiasm for Communism, while they still mistook it as a force for freedom, might have provided a powerful moral asset both among the Russian people and abroad. For their part the Nazis made use of Expressionist rhetoric in their political posters while denouncing Expressionist

Happy officers in a Moscow park: *Friends of Peace,* 1950, by S. Gelbergs (Sovfoto).

Happy, productive peasants: *Model Live-Stock Tender,* 1957, by Wei Chi-mei (Eastfoto).

121

paintings as degenerate. In relation to art, the instinct of totalitarianism is not to exploit modernism but to do away with it. To it the academy represents an aspiration toward High Culture, while the assertion of independent meanings by avant-garde art fills it with rage and Philistine hatred.

To the Communist, art is a weapon or a future luxury. Only when society has satisfied its material needs can it "afford" a free, that is, non-utilitarian, art. Hypnotized by the ideological function of art in earlier societies, Marxist totalitarianism is blind to the influence of art in democratic societies upon the dynamics of production and upon innovation in science and technology. To the commissar, the free artist is guilty of wasting materials and units of energy on the vanity of "self expression."

Philistine hatred of modern art reached its most feverish pitch in Nazi Germany, whose Führer was himself a bottom-grade illustrator and where the Academy had been the most firmly entrenched in Europe. Reinforced by the Party's dream and practice, Nazi art carried the academic ideal to the peak of brutal lumpishness. Soviet Socialist-Realism has tended for the main part, like academic art in the United States, to reflect the uncultivated idealism of a new ruling class that demands of art the flattering of authority, the beautification of life and the encouragement of laudable sentiments [see p. 121]. In contrast to the dull, well-intentioned technical skill of Soviet academicism, the academic art inherited by Hitler brought with it ferocious metaphysical am-

bitions far beyond those of a mere elevated trade. As the sculptor Kolbe, a "master" who prospered under the Nazis, put it in describing his *Zarathrustra:* "A high plane has therewith been entered . . . the great, powerful man who liberates himself, that was the task, that was also the way to my own freedom." Egomania of this sort is not inconsistent with Nazi servitude; it is heightened by slavery and made more concrete. The world-hunger of the German academician converted to Nazism vented itself in a malignant glamour that is on the verge of the super-real. The heroic figures of Nazi painting and sculpture seem born to carry on their faces a peevish emptiness aggressively directed, like Nazi politics itself, against every fact and idea of the twentieth century. A conscious ennobling of murder exists not too far below the surface in the works of these horrible professors dreaming of the heroic—I have not the slightest hesitation in stating that artists like Breker and Thorak should have been arraigned among the war criminals at Nuremberg [see p. 117].

Another revolting feature of Nazi art is its surpassed sex, "sublimated" in the exact dialectical meaning of the term; i.e., it is sex uplifted (*aufheben*) into something "higher" than the erotic yet retaining its original prurience. (The lady who photographed Breker's *The Victor* for the National Socialist publishing company took care to locate his penis in the exact diagonal center of her print, no doubt as an inspiration to German homosexuals and genetically-minded

Awesome monument (Mussolini atop Mussolini): *The Empire,* 1940, by Ferruccio Vecchi.

Awesome monument (Lenin atop wedding-cake): Model for the Palace of the Soviets, ca. 1939.

Portrait of the leader as a young poet:
The Duce, 1928, by Ettore di Giorgio.

Portrait of the leader as a young poet:
Comrade Stalin in 1905 by K. Merabichvili, 1938.

The founding fathers: *Marx and Engels*
in sugary marble, by Belosotsky.

housewives.) The male and female of Joseph Thorak [see p. 116], Nazidom's Number Two sculptor after Breker, with their smug self-righteous expressions, prim hairdos, heavy flesh, over-prominent but concealed sex, are perfect examples of the pornography of esthetic and ideological uplifting. Wilhelm Reich in his early *Mass Psychology of Fascism* provided rich data on the Nazi strategy of generating violence through aseptic obscenity.

Neither Fascist nor Soviet art achieved this degree of degradation. In Italy under Mussolini, goddesses, heroes, big-chested ethnic types, breedworthy naked girls, largely displaced the work of the experimental modernists. Yet Italian academicians were held in check by Italy's sincere longing for modernization, by the ideological slackness and relative lack of ferocity of Italian Fascism and by the tolerance displayed toward Futurists who had been patriotic precursors of the Black Shirts. As for Soviet art, the prudery of the Bolsheviks and their hostility to inherited myths inhibited the academic lust for symbolic nudes. Though Marx and Engels done up in plaster were converted into a pair of Olympians underwriting the crimes of the Leader in a manner equivalent to Hitler's eagle-launching Titan, at least they kept their sublimated clothes on [see left]. Only in Germany did the academic counter-revolution reveal itself in the full range of its tasteless and content-less grandeur, from man-gods to striptease genetical specimens, as the deadly foe of modern art, the modern world and life itself.

The Paris Opera, designed by Charles Garnier in a two-stage competition in 1860-61, but not completed until 1875, owes its peculiar brand of Second-Empire grandeur largely to the brilliant organization of its interior spaces. The great stair hall and the surrounding vestibules and corridors for the circulation of people and social gatherings during intermissions rival the scenographic splendor of the auditorium and even the stage.

XII

The Grand Opera

By John Jacobus

John Jacobus is the author of *Philip Johnson* and of *Twentieth-
Century Architecture: The Middle Years, 1940-65,* recently
published by Thames and Hudson in England. He is professor
of art history at the University of Indiana. His article on
Sir John Soane appeared in the 1967 Annual, *The Grand Eccentrics.*

It would not, perhaps, be included in anyone's choice for the seven architectural marvels of the known world. On the other hand, the Paris Opera would undoubtedly be cited towards the end of any connoisseur's list of the 40 or 50 representative structures of Western Civilization. Few buildings since its Second Empire heyday can equal its majesty: Wright's Imperial Hotel, Le Corbusier's Assembly Hall at Chandigarh, possibly the Eiffel Tower—or, in another vein, the Victor Emmanuel Monument—do no more than approach it. Revealingly, no single example of twentieth-century technology, be it skyscraper or arena, suspension bridge or rocket-launching structure, can match its special brand of grandeur. Like the Romantic piano concerto of the late nineteenth century, or, for that matter, grand opera itself, it is an extinct species, and most recent efforts to breathe new life into this virtuoso art of Opera House design have been something less than convincing.

If the species "Opera House" is extinct, so also is its genus of Beaux-Arts composition (to distinguish its design type from the merely "academic"). Quite literally, the Paris Opera is the last, and in a way the most vulnerable, of a brontosaurian race of buildings whose history reaches back to the High Renaissance. We are at once too close in time and yet too distant in our perceptions and sentiments to grasp easily its basic significance. Monuments of "late" periods have commonly suffered from disparaging art-historical judgments. The jibe of decadence is a thrust not easily parried: witness the fate (until recently) of Roman Imperial architecture or of the many species of late Gothic. Hence we are, today, too prone to see this monument thrown up by Na-

poleon III's Second Empire as chiefly, if not exclusively, a monument to that crinoline society.

In reality, this most sumptuous of Opera Theaters, designed by Charles Garnier as the result of a two-stage competition in 1860-61, was not inaugurated until 1875, five years after the utter collapse of that very Empire, the dispersal of its notables and, indeed, two years after the passing of Napoleon III himself. Moreover the gaudy display of colors, materials and shapes on the exterior as well as the interior is not truly representative of the popular academic trends of the time. Other public buildings contemporary with Baron Haussmann's ruthless if effective modernization of Paris— schools, churches, railroad stations, garrisons and the like— tend to be more restrained, harder in outline and with harsh, severe, if complicated decorative elaborations. Indeed, as late as 1909 an architectural historian of the *fin de siècle,* Luigi Callari, would describe Garnier's unique summa of academic expertise as "the gifted translation into stone of the restlessness and feverishness of modern life." Such views are hardly convincing today when, if admired at all, the Opera is seen as a mildly entertaining contrast to the hard-headedness of contemporary architectural theory and the insipidity of its application in routine works. If anything, the Opera is neither severe nor insipid.

The atypical luxuriance of the Paris Opera is not easily explained. True, the architect was partly responsible through his emulation of certain specific models, among them Michelangelo's Capitoline and Sansovino's Venetian Library. These types of Renaissance buildings were not frequently employed as models in mid-ninteenth-century Paris, where the more common paradigms were to be found in the French Classical traditions of the seventeenth and eighteenth century. Furthermore, this native tradition founded and perpetuated by the Mansarts, Gabriels and others had, since the time of Colbert, been institutionalized into a Royal Academy of Architecture, which, with changes in organization, has successfully survived the several revolutions and restorations from 1789 onwards.

Because of its remarkable survival coefficient, in a century when governmental regimes were impermanent and unstable, the Academy, in concert with the Ecole des Beaux-Arts, exerted a particularly reactionary force. Charles Garnier (1825-98) was in no way an exceptional or atypical product of this well-oiled if anachronistic educational machine, one which was unwilling and/or incapable of coming to terms with the emerging modern world. At the age of 15 he entered the *atelier* of Hippolyte Lebas, a *maître* whose pedagogical success can be measured by the large number of his students who were successful competitors for the Prix de Rome, an honor which Garnier duly won in 1848, having made an unsuccessful effort two years earlier. Otherwise he seems to have been an indifferent student, combining his studies at the Beaux-Arts with the task of earning a modest living as a draftsman in the *bureau* of Viollet-le-Duc, the pioneering medieval archeologist who at that time was deeply engrossed in the restoration of Notre-Dame. The one peculiar aspect of Garnier's apprentice years was his employment by the most vocal champion of a revived Gothic architecture at a time when the Academy was waging a last-ditch rhetorical stand against the Middle Ages. Moreover, the bad feelings between Viollet-le-Duc and the Academic pundits were destined to become even more violent with the passing of time. In 1863, with the aid of certain figures in the government, he made a determined assault upon the hallowed prerogatives of the Academy and the Ecole des Beaux-Arts which, if unsuccessful, was sufficiently virulent to poison relations among French architects of various tendencies for the remainder of the century. It was in this climate that Garnier's Opera was designed and constructed between 1861 and 1865, and it is worth noting that there is certainly no visible evidence of bitter controversy in this happiest and most radiant of academic designs. However, its popular success certainly prolonged the life of the controversy between the somnolent *anciens* and the rational activists of the Viollet-le-Duc camp, if only because that very success proved to be an elixir of youth for a moribund style and system. By its very renown, Garnier's Opera very likely postponed the arrival of a modern style in France in much the same way that the 1893 Columbian Exposition in Chicago suspended hopes for a new architecture in early twentieth-century America.

Garnier's sojourn at the Villa Medici in Rome, the recompense of his Grand Prix in '48, was supplemented by travel in Greece and Asia Minor, where he devoted much time to a study of the Temple at Aegina, whose "restoration" in the form of elaborate drawings represented one of his major student projects; it was sent back to Paris for the approbation of the Academy. These designs figured in the Salon of 1853, the Exposition Universelle of 1855, and they were published in 1858. Interestingly, these paper restorations emphasized, indeed exaggerated, the use of polychromy in antique monuments, inciting a reviewer to exclaim over his *"tons lourds et criards."* Returning to Paris, the young laureate-architect encountered the sort of mediocre fortune that was usually the lot of ex-Prix de Rome recipients during the remainder of their careers—his success came in the form of sinecures with the government rather than in opportunities to create new monuments. In 1858 he built a routine edifice in the newly opened Boulevard Sebastopol, the fees of which made possible another trip to Italy. Indeed, this escape from the city of Paris, then in the throes of reconstruction under the guidance of Haussmann, is virtually symbolic. Paradoxically, this era of febrile building activity was not conducive to much distinguished architectural design. Moreover Haussmann was not especially keen on leaving the big tasks of directing his work to architects; his techniques being more allied to executive fiat and the subtle provocation of private speculation on land values. An ambitious architect in Second Empire Paris could not really aspire to leadership on a creative level, but was forced to settle for a position in the bureaucracy or devote his energies to conniving for a seat among the *anciens* of the Academy, or *Institut* as it had come to be known. If he concentrated on design and construction, he found himself building mere façades along avenues laid out by others in authority.

There is no evidence leading us to conclude that the young Charles Garnier of this moment in time had aspirations any different from many of his contemporaries. Nor is there reason to think him more talented than a number of other footloose young architects of the day. As he himself would later admit, his success with the Opera competition was to a large degree a matter of fate or luck, and consequently his masterpiece a product as much of a system and its tradition as of personal inspiration. The site of the Opera was on a newly opened square adjacent to the Grands Boulevards, flanked by a lozenge-shaped criss-cross of new streets. One might reasonably suppose that the new streets were designed to conform with the new building, but in reality the opposite was the case, and Garnier's building was fitted onto a relatively predetermined, if "new," site in a once-residential area that was fast being transformed into an important commercial quarter. If this situation resulted in the building being rather cramped and hemmed in by other buildings of nearly equal height, nonetheless the Paris Opera became a vitally integrated monument at the center of urban action, a crown jewel in the fabric of the city, and not some extraneous, separate, isolated object in the manner of London's Royal Festival Hall or New York's Lincoln Center. In truth, Garnier's Opera would be infinitely poorer without the new city of

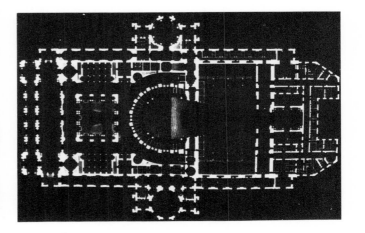

The façade of the Opera [top], probably inspired by municipal
theaters in French provincial cities but with a grandiloquence
corresponding to the importance of the building, looks out on
the intersection of the Grands Boulevards. It was designed
for a specified site within the lozenge of pre-existing streets
[above]. The plan [above right] shows the large proportion
of space allocated to access halls for circulation leading
to the auditorium itself, with stage beyond; the further end of the
building houses the Library. Garnier's drawing of the transverse
section [right] suggests a Bibiena-like architectural fantasy.

The Rennes Municipal Theater, built in 1835, exemplifies the general prototype of the façade of the Paris Opera.

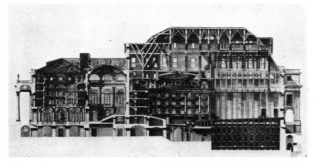

The transverse section of Victor Louis' great Neo-Classic theater in Bordeaux [above], 1780, a direct ancestor of Garnier's design for the Paris Opera [below].

The staircase of the Bordeaux theater, despite greater classic severity, was the clue to Garnier's conception.

squares and tree-lined boulevards, of an urban circulation system that sought to introduce the axial regularity of Le Nôtre's Versailles to the chaotic diversity of the pre-Second Empire city. On the other hand, the very nature of the newly regularized street system of Paris meant that very little need be demanded by way of distinction from the surrounding buildings, even those at the principal intersections. They rarely had a chance to score a point through individuality, and it is chiefly through grandeur rather than genre that the Paris Opera stands out in the urban context—with a helpful assist from its fortuitous location.

Like political elections in twentieth-century France, a second *scrutin* was necessary in order to identify a clear victor in the competition for the Opera during the winter and spring of 1860-61. Open competitions for the selection of an architect were not de rigueur at this time. In this case it was hardly more than an administrative afterthought meant, in the eyes of the well-informed, to achieve nothing more than the legitimizing of an already-agreed-upon nomination. In the fall of 1860, the architect who had caught the eye of the Empress Eugénie was none other than Viollet-le-Duc, an unlikely choice based upon his past experience as restorer, but a figure well supported by the denizens of the court. Dutifully he submitted his competition project along with those from 180 other competitors. Probably he believed that since his name had already been prominently mentioned among those few being considered for the prestigious task, rivals would not be inspired to enter the lists. Even after the decision had gone against him, he was constantly being badgered by hopeful contractors who naturally assumed that some intrigue would set aside the young unknown Garnier, who emerged from the second limited competition (from which Viollet-le-Duc had been excluded) as the victor by the end of May. But nothing of the sort was forthcoming.

The various competition projects that were published in professional journals at the time represent a fairly good index of the academic method of composition, with many designs making a special effort to distinguish on the exterior the interior functional differentiation between stage and auditorium. Equally, most designs paid considerable attention to the problem of multiple entries, often sheltered in one way or another, and the plans were often ingenious in the organization of interior circulation around vast stairs and foyers. Garnier's virtue was to have solved all these academic design problems with greater flourish. His stairs and corridors seem more commodious, and, what's more, are more spatially dramatic. Indeed, the grand stair with its surrounding gallery is so effective a setting for public as well as covert rendezvous that it far outshines the several circles of loges in the auditorium, both functionally and visually.

The basic problem of the design of a theater, of "the front of the house," is the gathering together of many people from several directions and installing them with more or

Viollet-le-Duc's competition projects for the Paris Opera [above and below], although lacking the flourish of Garnier's design, may have influenced the latter's final solution.

less comfort (depending upon the class of ticket held) in the smallest possible space. At the same time allowance must be made for the very special visitor (the Emperor, his guests and entourage), for whom altogether special measures of comfort and security are demanded, thus complicating circulation and services. The design of a theater may thus be conceived in terms of the movements of people before, after and during the intermissions of the spectacle, and it is here that Garnier gave his all. Indeed, it is in the solution of the circulation problem that the Beaux-Arts tradition was supreme. For a century a type of planning based on what might be called a circulation diagram was one of the most important aspects of architectural indoctrination at the Ecole. This technique placed great importance upon corridors, vestibules and great halls, the sole function of which was to give access to the often smaller and less grandiose working spaces of the building. From this planning philosophy comes the consequence that many monumental nineteenth-century structures are overburdened with much non-functional space in the form of gargantuan entries and passages. However, in the case of the Opera, the scenographic effects of the great stair had a function of the first order, since in a theater of this magnitude not one but two spectacles vied for attention. The audience itself was as visible in the auditorium (the house lights were not normally dimmed during a performance at this time) as the singers and dancers on the stage, and dressed accordingly. From this circumstance it follows that the Opera's circulation spaces were a kind of stage in themselves fit to accommodate a real-life parade of sumptuous colors and materials that could hardly be rivaled onstage. In fact, it is not far from the mark to see in the endless public spaces of Garnier's Opera the transformation of the illusionistic stage design of the Bibienas and their followers into a phantasmagoric architecture of real life.

In an article published in the *Gazette des Beaux-Arts* in 1876, Garnier flattered himself that he had not only been inspired by Michelangelo and Sansovino in the composition of his exterior features, but that he had improved upon them! More important as sources are certain other features, notably the layout. Here Garnier may have been influenced in the massing of his final project by certain features in the elevation of Viollet-le-Duc's design, notably the changes of scale and silhouette along the lateral façades. More certain is the inspiration that Garnier received from the layout and even the stair hall of Victor Louis' great Neo-Classic theater in Bordeaux. The unusual importance given to the public circulation areas in that design together with the shape and layout of the staircase were surely Garnier's starting point, from which he proceeded to spatial and decorative elaborations of a sort for which we must go back to the Bibienas and even to the young Piranesi to find an equal. The architecture of his own day could offer him very little, except insofar as the elaborate and unreal annual Grand Prix projects represented a petrification of many large-scale concepts

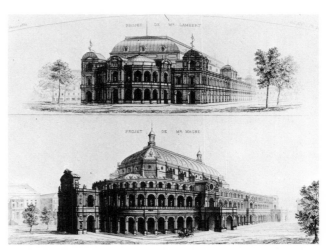

Faithful to academic formulas are a number of the other projects, many attempting to express interior functions on the exterior.

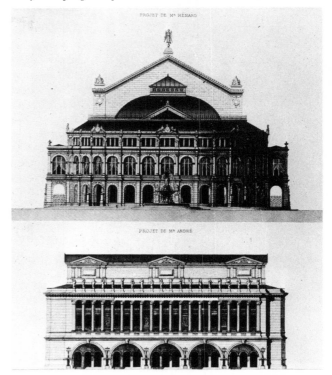

worked out in the late Baroque and Romantic Classic eras. In this respect, Garnier's masterpiece is really a distant and belated manifestation of the grandiloquent geometrical masses of Ledoux, Boullée and their contemporaries, allowances being made for the greater decorative elaboration which, in the 1860s and '70s was once again permissible if not altogether typical. Indeed, the élan of Garnier's decoration was seen by younger architects as one of the marks of the building's modernity. The designer of the Samaritaine department store (one of the monuments of the Parisian Art Nouveau), Frantz Jourdain, was a student during the period of the Opera's construction, and when he came to publish his memoirs in 1922 he testified to the fact that many at that time had hailed Garnier's design as a break from "the yoke of *pompiérisme*." No doubt some of its more unusual decorative features were a general inspiration for the designers of metal-framed department stores and exhibition buildings during the remainder of the century, and the twisting, languorous curves to be detected in the stair itself can properly be thought of as significant forerunners of the Art Nouveau.

On the exterior, Garnier's façade elevation, with an enormous loggia set on top of a relatively severe round-arched basement, owes nothing to the colonnaded type of façade favored by the Romantic-Classic architects in their own dream-like schemes, and in fact used by Victor Louis in Bordeaux. In a very general way, the elevation of the Paris Opera might have been inspired, as would those of many other competition projects, by a type of façade employed in municipal theaters in provincial cities like Rennes (1835; architect: Millardet) and Le Havre (1844; architect: Brunet-Debaines), but of course with an increase in bombast corresponding to an increase in size and capital importance. Interestingly enough, on the provincial level, theater architecture in France was never the same after Garnier. Numerous municipalities constructed local theaters that had the presumption to rival the decorative grandiloquence of the capital, with results that are as naïve as Angoulême (1866-72; architect: Antoine Soudée) or as suave as Montpellier (1884; architect: Cassien-Bernard). Significantly enough, the architect of Montpellier had learnt his trade in the *bureau* of Garnier. In Paris itself the new theaters of the boulevard, like the Renaissance (1872; architect: Charles de Lalande) aped the bombast of the Opera on a reduced scale, where earlier structures of this genre were built with no more pretention than the earlier provincial houses. And, on an international level, the influence of Garnier's Opera stretches from Prague to Palermo and ultimately to Mexico

Construction photographs of the Paris Opera [facing page] reveal that under the veneer of Garnier's decorative extravaganzas was employed an elephantine approach to modern construction which was destined to become obsolete.

The Angoulême theater [left], 1866-72, by Antoine Soudée, is a provincial attempt to rival the panache of the Paris Opera.

In Paris, the new theaters of the boulevards like La Renaissance, 1872, by Charles de Lalande, imitated Garnier's decorative elaborations.

The Montpellier theater, 1884, was built by Cassien-Bernard, who was trained in Garnier's office.

City. Indirectly this species of hysterically rejuvenated architecture (Academic Romanticism, if it must be named at all), influenced most of the world's fairs from Paris to Chicago, St. Louis and San Francisco down until World War I, at which point it vanishes almost without a trace. As for efforts that have recently been made to re-fashion a theater or opera-house architecture today, in the third quarter of the twentieth century, this is a complex matter related not only to the Garnier tradition but to other twentieth-century issues as well, and might well form the subject of a separate discussion.

The Paris Opera, sometimes known simply as the Palais Garnier (a not undeserved accolade for its designer), succeeded momentarily in pouring new wine into old bottles. The trouble was that while the new vintage seemed good when young, it didn't age especially well. The academic system sponsored by the Ecole des Beaux-Arts was incapable of producing anything more than an illusion of a new architecture. Indeed, all it produced after the mid-century was one super-monument, an authentic masterpiece to be sure, but a building that almost by its very nature could have no vital sequel, only pallid or whimsical derivatives. Indeed, the construction photographs with their revelation of the astounding yet totally concealed reliance upon metal-frame construction in the Paris Opera indicate how ill-suited this type of building was to the emergent technologies of the time.

We need not love it any the less for its failure to pledge loyalty and fealty to new materials and structural systems; the last of its race, Garnier's masterpiece cannot be faulted. Unfortunately, the active, alive tendencies of late nineteenth- and early twentieth-century architecture were forced to ally themselves to a new set of social, technical and esthetic realities which, if not totally removed from the achievements of the Romantic Century, were largely unrelated to the cul-de-sac into which Beaux-Arts architecture had carried itself, and within which Garnier was perfectly content to remain. His subsequent works, which in no way measure up to the accomplishment of his early youth (he was 36 when he won the opera competition), demonstrate the all-but-complete collapse of the academic system whose final flower he was. And finally, his bitter opposition to the construction and even preservation of the Eiffel Tower, the one monument of the *fin de siècle* which in its way manages to span the gulf between the Beaux-Arts past and the Cubist-Constructivist future, indicates the end of not just an era, but an epoch in history reaching back to the time of Colbert and beyond.

XIII

The Orthodox Master

By Wen Fong

Head of graduate programs in Oriental art at Princeton,
Prof. Fong is largely responsible for the spectacular acquisitions
in his field at the university's museum in recent years.

This article is based on a section in the author's forthcoming book,
*Wang Hui and the Great Synthesis: Based on Ten Works by the
Master in the Collection of Mr. and Mrs. Earl Morse.* This collection
of paintings by Wang Hui will be presented to the Princeton Museum.

In 1691, Wang Hui was summoned to the court of the Emperor K'ang-hsi (1662-1722) to supervise the creation of the "Southern Inspection Tour" (*Nan-hsün t'u*) scrolls, which were to illustrate and commemorate the Emperor's Southern journey of 1689. By Chinese count—which considers a child at birth as one year old—the master had just turned 60 that year. During the previous 30 years, he had built up an enormous reputation in Chiang-nan in Southern China. He was referred to as the "painting sage" who had realized the "Orthodox" ideal of achieving a "Great Synthesis" (*ta-ch'eng*) of all the earlier styles of the Sung and Yüan periods. His mentor, Wang Shih-min (1592-1680), himself a leading master, described him as "the kind of painter who has not been seen for 500 years."

A typical example of Wang Hui's work as a court painter in the 1690s is the large *Winter Landscape,* which is signed in the lower right corner in four carefully written characters: "Wang Hui respectfully painted." The large painting is pleasant, but mechanical. It uses a familiar Northern Sung formula repeated not only by himself, but also by his followers. The composition is cluttered with descriptive details and tortuous decorative passages. The brushwork is dry and astringent. Wang Hui, in short, painted this not from his heart, but for popular consumption. He was painfully aware

Left: Detail reveals the ink tones and the archaic "seal-style" brushstrokes of Wang Hui's masterpiece of "academic" calligraphic abstraction, *Imitating Wu Chen's "Summer Mountains"* [see p. 139]. Collection Mr. and Mrs. Earl Morse, New York.

of his failure. On seeing one of his earlier works in 1701, he lamented: "I am old. My years are spent. [Such is] the difficulty of the Tao of painting. The harder one pursues it, the more elusive it becomes!"

In truth, Wang Hui had probably painted his most brilliant works a full decade before he entered into the Emperor's service. We would certainly remember him as an artist of the first order had he, like Wang Shih-min, died in 1680. Few Chinese artists' lives ran so straight and were so totally dedicated as Wang Hui's. By the time he was 30, he already personified Tung Ch'i-ch'ang's ideal of a "scholar painter who learned to exhaust the limits of workmanship and refinement, making Creation his teacher and friend." In the 1670s, his closest friend Yün Shou-p'ing wrote: "I have witnessed Wang Hui's painting undergo several metamorphoses [*pien*] . . . With each metamorphosis, it arrives at a new summit." When the brilliant student became a successful teacher, metamorphosis ceased.

The "Orthodox" theory of painting propounded by Tung Ch'i-ch'ang (1555-1636) in the closing years of the sixteenth and the beginning of the seventeenth century was a revolutionary doctrine directed against the ailing, decorative conventions of late Ming art. By reverting to ancient models, Tung sought to restore to landscape painting its ancient simplicity and truthfulness. Painting was turned, in theory, into a humanistic discipline. A "Great Synthesis" of all the ancient styles was proposed to represent the perfect sum, as it were, of all the perfect parts. Technically, Tung equated painting with calligraphy, insisting that the chief desideratum in painting was brushwork and form rather than repre-

The Orthodox Master

sentation. In the handscroll *Landscape in the Style of Huang Kung-wang,* painted before 1610, Tung reduces Huang Kung-wang's brush idiom to a calligraphic formula of "[filling] concave and convex forms [with] straight texture strokes." Landscape forms are turned into abstract graphic patterns. These he manipulates, as formal elements, according to his compositional principles of "void and solid," "rising and falling" and "opening and closing." As an over-all concept, he uses the ancient calligraphic principles of *shih* or kinesthetic movement. Continuous "breath-movements" circulate through the interconnected landscape forms. These "breath-movements" represented, for Tung and his followers, "life-motion" in landscape painting.

Born in 1632 in Ch'ang-shu (modern Kiangsu province), Wang Hui was discovered in 1651 by Wang Chien (1598-1677), who soon introduced him to the great master of Loutung, Wang Shih-min. The young man's brilliance so startled Wang Shih-min at their first meeting that the latter was moved to exclaim: "This is my teacher! How could he make me *his* teacher?" At Wang Shih-min's country villa in the western suburbs of T'ai-ts'ang, Wang Hui was given the opportunity to study and imitate all the ancient paintings in Wang Shih-min's rich collection. As Wang Hui's artistic stature grew, Wang Chien and Wang Shih-min magnanimously played the roles of ardent admirers of, and commen-

Wang Hui, late in life, retired into an official, decorative style: *Winter Landscape,* 1690s, ink, slight color on silk (67½ inches high). Morse collection.

Right: By the propounder of "Orthodox" theories, Tung Ch'i-ch'ang: *Landscape in the Style of Huang Kung-wang,* late 1600s, ink on paper (15 inches high). Cleveland Museum.

Old-master model for the new theoreticians: Huang Kung-wang's *Dwelling in the Fu-ch'un Mountains,* 1350, ink on paper (13 inches high). National Palace Museum, Taiwan.

Model, copier and copier reinterpreted: the Northern Sung master Chü-jan's *Snow Scene* [left], ca. 960-980, Palace Museum, Taiwan, is the original of Wang Shih-min's copy of the 1620s, Central Museum, Taiwan, which in turn inspired his protégé Wang Hui's *Imitating the Brushwork of Chü-jan*, 1664, Morse collection.

tators on, the younger man's art. The extant writings of the two older Wangs in fact consist almost entirely of eulogistic colophons that they inscribed on Wang Hui's paintings.

The "metamorphosis" of Wang Hui's style through the 1660s and 1670s may best be studied in a series of paintings (in the collection of Mr. & Mrs. Earl Morse, New York) executed in the style of the tenth-century master Chü-jan. Chü-jan, according to the "Orthodox" theory of landscape painting, was one of the "patriarchs" of the "Southern School," which produced the "Four Great Masters of the Yüan Period," Huang Kung-wang, Wu Chen, Ni Tsan and Wang Meng. A hanging scroll by Wang Hui, titled *Imitating the Brushwork of Chü-jan,* dated 1664, reflects the composition of the *Snow Scene* attributed to Chü-jan. Wang Hui's immediate model, however, was Wang Shih-min's copy of the *Snow Scene* in the "Small Sketches" (*Hsiao-chung hsien-ta*) album—an album which Wang Hui faithfully studied in the 1660s and '70s. Freely adapting elements from Wang Shih-min's sketch, Wang Hui enlarged the group of pine trees in the foreground on the left, linking it diagonally with the smaller pine forest in the middle-distance, which in turn he related rhythmically with the great serpentine movement of the central peak in the background. In the drawing of the mountain form, Wang Hui followed Tung Ch'i-ch'ang's graphic formula of "filling the outlines with straight texture strokes." Individual brushstrokes are now the sole conveyor of life and energy; they grow and expand continuously until the whole becomes a great flowing pattern of undulating ed-

dies and counter-eddies, serving to "move" peaks and valleys around. Wang Hui wrote: "I must use the brush and ink of the Yüan to move the peaks and valleys of the Sung, and fuse with this the breath-resonance of the T'ang. I will then have a work of the Great Synthesis." The billowing movement in the composition is called the "dragon vein" (*lung-mo*). It creates an all-inclusive over-all effect, denying the compartmentalized division of the Northern Sung. The new compositional unity depends not so much on the balance and harmony of the parts, as on the kinetic energy and tension created by the individual strokes within the total structure.

A new model was used in Wang Hui's *Imitating Chü-jan's 'Floating Mist Rising over Distant Peaks,'* dated 1672. The painting shows a great heaving mountain mass with round calligraphic strokes in interlocking patterns of arcs, circles and dots. The only vertical elements in the painting are the trees in the lower portion of the composition; these are used merely to indicate the direction of the "dragon veins." Colophons by the artist and by his teachers Wang Shih-min and Wang Chien, found on the top of the painting, record the excitement of the new stylistic discovery. "This painting," writes Wang Hui, "does not make use of any paths, issuing streams, houses, temple buildings, boats or bridges. It depends solely on broad and heroic *shih* [compositional forces]." Wang Shih-min finds that "a primal breath fills the composition," and Wang Chien calls the painting "a living incarnation of Chü-jan." The actual model is lost, but a replica of it, now titled *Seeking the Tao*

Attributed to Chü-jan (ca. 960-980): *Seeking the Tao in Autumn Mountains*, ink, light color on silk (61½ inches high; National Palace Museum, Taiwan), replica of lost model for Wang Hui's scroll [right].

Wang Hui's *Imitating Chü-jan's "Floating Mist Rising Over Distant Peaks,"* dated 1672, ink on silk (76 inches high). Morse collection.

The Orthodox Master

in the Autumn Mountains, still exists. Wang Hui's encounter with such a model in 1672 was a revelation: the "Southern School" style, epitomized by this "Chü-jan," treats painting as an orchestration of calligraphic lines in abstract space. The discovery provided Wang Hui with the key to interpret all the "Southern School," Chü-jan-derived styles. He was now able to "write out" his "Huang Kung-wangs," "Wu Chens" and "Wang Mengs" in the same calligraphic idiom.

An album by Wang Hui, dedicated to Wang Shih-min in 1673, offers a brilliant manifesto of the seventeenth-century

"Orthodox" belief in the "Great Synthesis" of Sung and Yüan styles. The album, in which a total of 11 different styles of the Sung and Yüan periods are represented, opens with an abbreviated statement of the "Chü-jan" style. The composition, which reverts to the ancient ideographic symbol of a "host" peak flanked by two "guest" peaks, is repeated not only in Kung Hsien's sketchbook of the 1670s, but also in the *Mustard Seed Garden Painter's Manual,* which was illustrated by Wang Kai, a pupil of Kung Hsien, and published in 1679. Not only are there no houses or figures, but also no trees or grass; there is not a single distracting detail. The *Mustard Seed* says of this composition: "There is no need for additional scenic details. The absence of such details makes the painting appear particularly deep and massive. This is what is known as 'treating the basic subject without embellishment.'"

Out of this "Chü-jan" calligraphic abstraction came many of Wang Hui's Southern School metamorphoses during this period. His copy of Huang Kung-wang's *Fu-ch'un Mountains* composition, dated 1673, is based on this "Chü-jan" formula. A small hanging scroll, *Imitating Wu Chen's "Summer Mountains,"* dated 1675, is a fully realized masterpiece in this style. The brushwork, round energy lines in circular rhythmic patterns, is highly abstract. The tip of every stroke is carefully centered and "hidden," so as to emulate the blunt and archaic look of the "seal style" calligraphy. The ink tones are rich and luminous. The design seems to have been spun out of a single revolving breath. The lively, pulsating "dragon vein" dominates. At the sides, rocks, trees and even houses are tilted, as if pulled towards the center by a tremendous centripetal force, creating a great vortex in the lower half of the painting. The outer circle of this pattern continues upward and turns into a greater counter-whorl in the mountain peak above. In the upper right corner of the painting, Wang Chien writes this appreciative colophon: "Tung

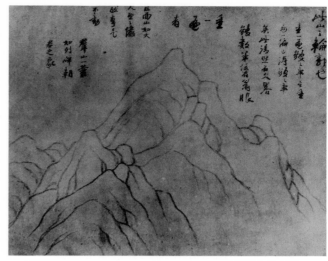

Further stylization of the past: album drawing attributed to Kung Hsien (active 1660-1700), one of 18 leaves, ink on paper (9¾ inches high).

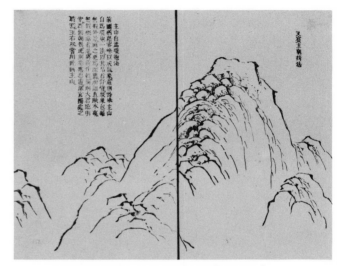

Ultimate stylization of the past: plate from *The Mustard Seed Garden Painter's Manual*, 1679, by Wang Kai (active 1680-1700): the text prescribes methods for every phase of art from inks to inspiration. Princeton University.

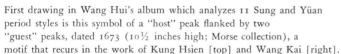

First drawing in Wang Hui's album which analyzes 11 Sung and Yüan period styles is this symbol of a "host" peak flanked by two "guest" peaks, dated 1673 (10½ inches high; Morse collection), a motif that recurs in the work of Kung Hsien [top] and Wang Kai [right].

Ch'i-ch'ang used to say to me that 'painters who possess beauty and elegance frequently lack fullness of strength; those who have power and vigor are often short of style and resonance.' Only in Wang Hui are all the desirable qualities present. It may be said that not a single hair in his work ever causes regret. This painting is deep and calm, and quietly aloof. A primal breath seems to flow spiritedly through it. It is one of his great masterpieces, and should be carefully treasured."

In seventeenth-century China, the "Orthodox" mind appreciated originality only when it was presented in the guise of tradition. Change or "metamorphosis" was valued not for its own sake, but as a process of renewal by which the traditional principles were continuously given new life and meaning. Discussing the problem of imitating ancient models, Tung Ch'i-ch'ang asserted that "whereas copying is easy, spiritual communion with an old master is difficult to achieve." The fact is that creative activity in the "Orthodox" sense, though stemming from the inner recesses of the human soul, was in no way egotistical; the "Orthodox" painter surrendered himself to his heritage so that he might be born and revealed again as part of its glory.

In the early works by Wang Hui, brush idioms borrowed from revered ancient sources were used to create powerful new forms. The novelty of the form, however, was in itself of no great significance. Since the Tao was considered eternal and unchanging, it followed that skillful execution was prized above new ways of doing things. There was a religious or ritualistic intensity in the early Wang Hui, whose powerful creative impulse was deliberately channeled into a given range of possibilities. In a work such as *Imitating Wu*

Chen's "Summer Mountains," we experience the force of the artist's conviction and his exaltation before his heritage. Such a painting finally transcends the stylistic problems of representation or abstraction, originality or imitation; it becomes a symbol, first, of man's mastery of his cultural heritage, and secondly, of his success in reconciling ancient conventions with living reality. The appreciative colophons of Wang Shih-min and Wang Chien, therefore, used a language that is more esthetic than descriptive. Both older men saw a "primal breath" in Wang Hui's works, and they spoke of "beauty and elegance" and "fullness of strength," "power and vigor" and "style and resonance." These words described not only the paintings, but also the man behind them. The familiar subjects Wang Hui painted thus belonged both to the "Orthodox" heritage and to living individuals. They are not only beautiful, but they are also deeply expressive of the innermost feelings and the esthetic values of the "Orthodox" scholar.

Indeed Wang Hui's success as an "Orthodox" master was so complete that even his failures in later years illustrated the pitfall of the "Orthodox" theory. While expounding the virtue of imitating the ancients, Tung Ch'i-ch'ang warned that true correspondence could only come about through divine metamorphosis. This metamorphosis kept the painter in a constant state of tension and exaltation. When, after Wang Shih-min's death in 1680, Wang Hui became an established master and teacher, his art visibly relaxed. His forms lost their force as he began to teach them as conventions. The later Wang Hui failed, in short, not because he persisted in the strenuous path of imitating the ancients, but rather because he yielded to the temptation of imitating himself.

In Wang Hui's *After Huang Kung-wang's "Dwelling in the Fu-ch'un Mountains"* [see p. 134], 1673, ink on paper (15⅛ inches high; Freer Gallery, Washington, D.C.), he imparts the "life-motion" of "Orthodox" theory to a composition based on an old-master model.

In *Imitating Wu Chen's "Summer Mountains"* [detail p. 132], 1675, ink on paper (26½ inches high; Morse collection),
Wang Hui is inspired to break the log-jam of academic codifications and release an over-all vortical energy.

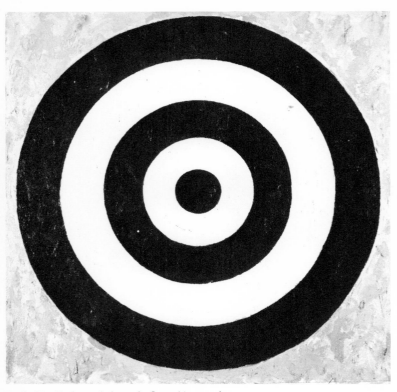

Partly Neo-Dada symbol, partly flat, arbitrary scheme
for painterly touches of encaustic: Jasper Johns'
Target, 1958 (36 inches square). Collection the artist.

Target becomes a format for pure stained color:
Kenneth Noland's *Toward Yellow,* 1961
(60 inches square). Collection the artist.

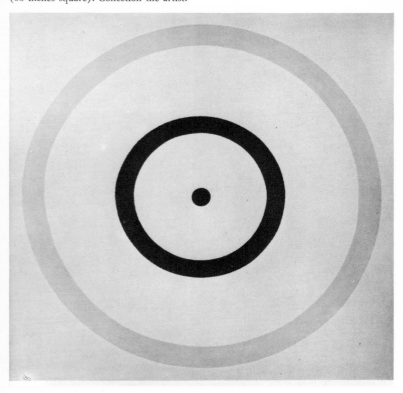

Thin concentric circles used as an intensifying
device for optical vibrations: Tadasky's *A-101,* 1964
(52 inches square). Museum of Modern Art, New York.

XIV

Is There a New Academy?

By Elizabeth C. Baker

A vulgar, but still surprisingly common reaction to this question is that all modern art is academic—that it fabricates clichés, imitates itself, is obsessed with self-perpetuating conventions and propagates a demand for spurious experimentation. This is often thought to take place because of conspiratorial maneuverings which are in their own way equivalent to the authoritarian academic bureaucracies of the past. While such an estimation of the events of this century is grotesquely distorted, there is nevertheless partial substance to it, as evidenced by the growing unwieldy machinery of the contemporary art world and the commercial exploitation of certain styles; in addition, such phenomena as the Venice Biennale (itself dating from the days of the old academies) and all its newer versions, with their faintly absurd solemnity, have become our surrogate Salons. Altogether, the problem bears examination.

It could be approached through multi-faceted definitions of academism, which would themselves be marvelously academic. Or, if our idea of academism comes to us mainly from nineteenth-century France, with connotations of an official, state-sponsored, arbitrarily imposed system, with its own iron-clad regime for teaching and perpetuating certain principles, then the question can be disposed of quickly—obviously there is no new academy.

For more than a century, advanced art movements have

developed almost entirely outside the old-fashioned academic establishments, and today's art world is so unlike what academies once were that only a ghost of them remains. Certainly our present "National Academies" and other vestigial official bodies are hardly relevant.

Modern art has turned increasingly inward, deprived of potentially stabilizing external factors (an accepted social or religious function, etc.), stimulated and tormented by seemingly infinite possibilities and at the same time by an absence of either tradition or obligation. Today's art has become a specialized, sometimes abstruse language, evolving primarily through its own internal, erratic, immensely inventive and ambitious aims.

The only appearance in this century of a powerful new academy was the Bauhaus. Founded on a revolutionary theory of what art would have to become to integrate itself with life in the machine age, it had a coherent pedagogical structure and a compelling ideology. However, though the Bauhaus was influential in architecture and design, it was antipathetic to the individualistic currents prevailing in the fine arts (a distinction the Bauhaus abhorred). What an artist is, and does, became an issue: having since the Renaissance dissociated himself from his unassuming medieval status as artisan-craftsman, having developed his position as an intellectual (an aspiration which various early academies were formed to promote), the modern artist was not willing to subject himself to the utilitarian dogma promulgated by the Bauhaus.

Though traditional academies have now practically disappeared, styles do not cease to gain adherents, critics do not cease to support certain artists or movements at the expense of others, museums do not cease to promote what they have a stake in—centers of power and influence, in other words, form as actively as ever. The webs of intertwined affinities and loyalties, professional and personal, are intricately spun. Possibilities for academic configurations in today's art world exist, if one wishes to see them there.

In broad terms, a case can be made for considering any extensive, influential art movement a kind of an academy, because by its very nature it tends to solidify, gain momentum, perpetuate itself and eventually become rigid before the necessity to reinvent asserts itself. In the process, it is likely to impede other tendencies, deprive them of public attention or immediate rewards and a favorable climate for development. And from the vantage point of artists shunted to one side, the influential "academy" will appear a threat.

However, an academy can also stand for a constructive situation, where wide-spread interest stimulates activity.

Real "movements," such as Cubism, Surrealism or Abstract-Expressionism, are important. With our current tendency to emphasize individual talent, one can forget the value of a broader effort. (Truly individual art is no more possible than truly collective art.) Continuity is essential; entirely individualistic invention (if it were possible) would equal chaos. Solitary explorers cannot work in a vacuum. The elaboration and development of their ideas by followers is significant both as a context for their own accomplishments and as a plateau for the launching of later work. Important art-historical periods have always involved strong movements. They do not necessarily "wear out" any faster than styles pursued only by a few.

But if we can conceivably use "academy" to designate one of these areas of prolific generative activity, the adjective "academic" is a more slippery term: though of course there is good academic and bad avant-garde work, "academic" generally has come to signify a kind of art which is stereotyped, unoriginal in conception, deriving from available recipes, from someone else's conclusions rather than fresh formulations.

The word has other implications too: an innovating artist can become academic, if he begins to imitate his own style. Yet this is a problematical application, because compulsive or automatic change can also be viewed as academic.

There is an academism of students or very young artists— it is natural for them to progress from imitation to their own decisions and inventions. An academic basis for their beginnings may be preferable. This should certainly be distinguished from academism in mature artists.

Critics are noticeably apt to become academic. Often, after establishing themselves as spokesmen for certain segments of the avant-garde, they become unreceptive to further change, fretful about tendencies outside of their preferred purlieus, settling down in one area as resident codifiers or propagandists.

There are also certain theories and practices which seem to produce academic results. Much twentieth-century art derived from a sentimentalizing mystique about modern life has a facile attractiveness which verges on sterility. A great deal of kinetic and light art and electronically-inspired, committee-produced extravaganzas, for example, are run-of-the-mill, formula-derived results of combining new materials with simple mechanical effects. They have in common with older academism in its debased phases an over-dependence on anecdotal allusion and an underdeveloped sense of form.

Probably the most prevalent academism we have today is that of the huge provincial would-be avant-garde. The art

Donald Judd's industrially fabricated aluminum box is factual, featureless, obtrusive—and classical: Untitled sculpture, 1965 (40 inches high). Collection Mr. and Mrs. Robert Scull.

A set of grey fiberglass tapered off-cubes by Robert Morris, 1965 (each 24 inches high), project enigma and metaphysical provocation. Castelli Gallery.

press, along with the mass mediums, substitutes for the old-fashioned teaching academy, supplying pre-digested, incomplete information that is picked up and emulated devotedly. The results are depressingly evident in hundreds of university art departments, regional, national and international exhibitions. Geographical provinciality in the visual arts is a very real thing, because of the necessity for first-hand contact with the real sources.

As "academic" has altered its meaning to a vague, derogatory description of any entrenched situation, every style of recent years has been accused of being an academy—this is true of more or less recognizable phases such as Pop, Hard-Edge, Op, Primary Structures, etc., as well as less defined categories grouped according to techniques (Assemblage, Kinetics, Shaped Canvas, color staining).

The concept can become ridiculously elastic: Abstract-Expressionism is supposed to have turned academic as it became accepted; Pop was called academic because its subject matter appealed to middle-class tastes and because of its relatively heavy reliance on literary content; Op was called academic because it could be derived so easily from formulas; and various kinds of representational painting are called academic because of ties to the figurative traditions of the past.

Yet, since the break-up of Abstract-Expressionist domination, it *has* sometimes seemed that we were witnessing the constant multiple births of mini-academies, whose ideas seemed momentarily all-pervasive, then exhausted themselves faster than before. Fear is often expressed that fads, fashions or novelties have come to substitute for "real" art. However this is a marginal consideration, related less to art than to its publicity.

It is also frequently asked whether change itself, or avant-gardism for its own sake, has not become a motivating force

so taken for granted that a new kind of academism results. Much can be enumerated to justify these qualms: many artists are driven to invent a new motif, look or theme for each one-man appearance—ideas seem to wear out quicker than they did. On the institutional side, museums often attempt to codify trends before they are half-way mature. (This can have a paralyzing instead of stimulating effect. A case in point was the Modern Museum's Op show, which turned out to be a scholarly, encyclopedic funeral.) Familiar, too, are dealers and collectors who abandon established artists for the new young, and all kinds of enterprises which search avidly for the latest. Even serious critics may get caught up in the game, telling artists what needs to be "solved" next. At any given moment, there are many aimless artists waiting to be magnetized by some compelling idea. The efficiency of publicity mechanisms simplifies the game of follow-the-leader, and all the imitators and provincials lend temporary weight to each fluctuation. All of this can be dangerous and potentially destructive, and is very much a part of the current art-world pattern.

Yet to deduce a coercive academism is to misconstrue broader aspects of the picture. First of all, the ephemeral

Tony Smith's *Die*, black 6-foot steel cube, has a ponderous, monumental, grim presence. Fischbach Gallery.

Ronald Bladen's untitled wood structure to be made in metal, 1966 (8 feet high), creates unease through its odd tilt off the floor. Fischbach Gallery.

143

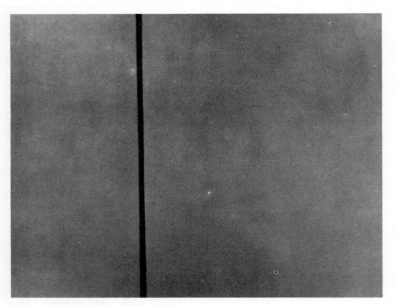

A single vertical stripe in a vibrant color field aims toward the sublime: Barnett Newman's *Tundra*, 1950 (72 inches high). Collection Mr. and Mrs. Robert Rowan.

Cooled, classicized painterliness: Morris Louis' *Burning Stain*, 1961 (87½ inches high), is a column of poured colors soaked into raw canvas. Collection University of Nebraska.

Is There a New Academy?

quality of the styles of the early '60s is basically a deception. Rather than whole categories of form which have run their course and died, there have been overlapping phases, frequently in close relation to one another. The glib verdict that the recent past has been a kind of visual vaudeville obscures important continuities which are now emerging—already this period looks less fragmented than it did. For instance, now that extraneous imitators have dropped away, it is clear that the major figures who promulgated Pop (which is supposed to be "finished") continue to do good work directly related to, and growing out of their "famous" periods. This is only one example of fertile areas which continue to produce with less fanfare, but no less effectiveness, than they did.

Actually, what exists is a complex, open, variegated simultaneity. Most post-Abstract-Expressionist styles have not been opposites, but complements, and most of them have not disappeared. Enormous unevenness of quality has been much greater than really definable separateness of aims and results.

Furthermore, the new institutions tailored to the avant-garde hardly qualify as academies in themselves, either individually or collectively, in spite of their obvious tendencies to do the same thing. Conspicuous as they are, they tend to be comparatively passive, responsive to the constantly shifting currents produced by artists. Not only are these institutions unable to direct or dictate, but they suffer from an inability to differentiate qualitatively. A sharp look at what is acquired, published, etc., usually shows a lack of discrimina-

tion that is quite astonishing. (This will probably get worse as patrons and "Friends" of museums play a more active part in acquisitions policies.) Few establishment organizations have shown a consistent taste or preference. By championing change and giving it their cachet, they simply reflect a broad spectrum of what is happening.

The effect of all this on artists and their work is basic in considering whether or not the current institutional emphasis on souped-up evolution truly represents an academic situation. One of its extraordinary aspects is how little the serious artist actually seems touched by it, beyond a generalized stimulation. While many artists are undoubtedly swayed by their observations of how others are "making it," and while an atmosphere of hectic competition prevails, there is, as always, a degree of inevitability to serious artistic development. A few innovators set their own pace and their own directions, a few perceptive critics elaborate, and everything else is secondary.

Today's advanced art is neither slick nor easy. Bear-hugs of sporadic approval do not seem to smother its unpredictability and unmanageability. Paradoxically, many artists tend to treat their work and ideas cavalierly, cutting away, abandoning, destroying—or at least violating what is expected of them. The negative intent intrinsic to much twentieth-century art persists. As for making an art suitable for museums, this certainly happens, but for every maker of handsome, oversized "museum pieces," there are many more who produce "impossibilities"—too big, too small, too perishable, too technological, too fragile—or who stop making collectable

Frank Stella's *The Marriage of Reason and Squalor*, 1959
(90¾ inches high), is an early, drastic assertion of
the painting-as-object idea. Museum of Modern Art, New York.

Vertical stripes carry contrapuntal color progressions
at a nearly environmental scale: Gene Davis' *Cardinal
Cadence*, 1964 (93 inches high). Poindexter Gallery.

art at all. And while a lot of recent art in a monumental
vein is ideally public, it is so unwieldy as to be far from a
curator's or collector's dream.

An avant-garde does, of course, still exist today (despite
reports of its absorption into "the scene"), but it is hardly
so accepted or comfortable as to enjoy (or suffer from) academic status. One has only to observe the various kinds of
conservative arts which flourish, including excellent landscape and figure painting, or the hostility to the continuing
sorties of experimenters. The concept of avant-gardism has
not lost its meaning simply because a faintly sophisticated
public is beginning to develop. The politico-moralist, cov-
ertly elitist position that an avant-garde can no longer exist
because it has an audience is absurd.

Altogether, recent kaleidoscopic shifts are signs both of vitality and unrest, not of academism; they are the product of
internal (artist-originated) rather than external (institutional) forces. The restless rate of invention is, if anything,
the source of the art world's over-stimulation, rather than the
reverse. In any case, the ambition to do unique, original,
new work is hardly peculiar to our own period, but has been
characteristic of most sophisticated, self-conscious periods in
history.

All this seems to preclude an academic hardening of the
situation at present.

Nevertheless there are certain current tendencies which may
be candidates for consideration as new academies, in the
sense that they represent powerful concentrations of forms

and ideas, somewhat organized for self-propagation. They
seem to be evolving differently now than in the interim
phases of the early '60s.

One of these is the color-stain school of painting, the formation of which, partially catalyzed by one critic, has been
a fascinating spectacle. This stylistic direction has produced
some of the best painting of recent years, particularly in the
case of Morris Louis. However, despite an attempt to legiti-
mize it in large group shows and by incessant elucidation as
the necessary inheritor of the prestige of Abstract-Expressionism, only three or four core members of the group seem
to hold much significance. Able followers have been few.

It is perhaps more interesting (more presumptuous, too,
considering its tenuous stage of evolution at this moment—
May, 1967) to examine the so-called Primary Structure activity, and the related Minimal art. This axis already is quite
impressively developed in terms of the level of accomplishment of a few of its leaders, and also in terms of sheer number.

Its momentum is due in part to its involvement in a twentieth-century mainstream, that of pure formal investigation;
it has been bolstered by wide interest from both artists and
critics. At the same time it has been relatively unexploited
by commercial promotion and presents itself with a lofty,
High-Art seriousness.

Starting in the late '50s, evolving unobtrusively from such
diverse sources as Johns, Noland, Stella, Judd, Morris and
others, with Barnett Newman as an important ancestor, the
work did not seem particularly homogeneous. Related aims

Josef Albers has used the same format of squares for years in infinitely varied color permutations: *Homage to the Square: Aurora,* 1951-55 (40 inches square). Janis Gallery.

Black square with a nearly invisible cruciform is half mystical, half specific vehicle for "art-as-art dogma": Ad Reinhardt's *Abstract Painting,* 1964 (60 inches square). Parsons Gallery.

Is There a New Academy?

became more apparent with the accretion of followers. By 1965, common tendencies were distinctly noticeable, the 3-dimensional wing having become surprisingly prolific. By the time of the 1966 "Primary Structure" show at the Jewish Museum, New York, and the "Systemic Painting" show at the Guggenheim, and in conjunction with rather different streams coming from England, it had expanded greatly. In the 1966–67 season it was a dominant, often repetitious note in the galleries and also, according to many artists who teach, a compelling attraction for students. Numerous museum shows with elaborate catalogue essays attempted to define it. The crest of this particular wave seems still to be rising.

There are certain ways in which this Primary-Minimal axis parallels the first academies (which were themselves informal associations of young artists of avant-garde leanings), or various other phases of later academies. To recognize such factors is not to say that Primary or Minimal art itself is academic in a derogatory sense. It is, rather, of interest that certain kinds of art seem to lend themselves to development within a somewhat academically structured situation.

(To consider this purist art of the '60s in academic or non-academic terms is to take an exaggeratedly particular point of view, it goes without saying. A different perspective is gained by seeing it in a Classic-Romantic polarity, as a classicizing of Abstract-Expressionist Romanticism.)

Primary-Minimal art *is* predominantly classicizing, ideal, formal; its geometry restricts personal extravagance. Neat in execution, it may be obsessively meticulous. Final results generally have to be pre-calculated; for industrially fabricated structures, the reason is obvious; but arbitrarily preselected figurations prevail in the paintings too. There are no traces of evolution, decisions, mistakes, changes; even in the paintings, personal sensual touch is more or less excluded. (The art of past academies has generally been classic, meticulous in finish, pre-planned through many preliminary stages, traces of which are suppressed in the final product.)

As visible craftsmanship is played down, the artist-as-intellectual takes on particular importance (another characteristic of past academism). Arbitrary, prior decisions, often stemming from theoretical hypotheses, seem glamorous. (The artists themselves say, "I don't need a studio any more, all I need is a telephone booth." Or, "I have managed to eliminate the work element from what I do.")

Aware of the theoretical implications of their work, these artists are also polemicists, like the critics who defend them. Didactic, contentious and evangelistic propensities are evident. (Academies have always tried to clarify, explain, promote, teach, convert.)

As was generally true of the erudite nature of much past academic work, the Primary-Minimal output requires a de-

Muted color borders a grey, vaporous square with shifting implications of space: Ralph Humphrey's *Wellington*, 1964-65 (70 inches square). Bykert Gallery.

Jo Baer's white canvas, 1965 (48 inches square), outlined in black and a thin color band, is less "minimal" than it seems, since it is part of a series hung in fixed positions. Fischbach Gallery.

gree of knowledge on the part of the viewer to be fully understood. Though comprehensible in concrete, physical terms, it is in a sense an art for informed insiders.

Along with its critical superstructure of dogma and explication has come a kind of historical pedigree which creates an aura of legitimacy. The new work is promulgated in such a way as to seem inevitable. It is seen as issuing not so much from Constructivist, Suprematist, Bauhaus or Neo-Plastic sources (most of which are repudiated), as obliquely but organically from Abstract-Expressionism, from which come its scale, drama, daring and the personal oddity that give it a different look and feel from its geometric predecessors. (The academies of the past also considered themselves the heirs of an historical succession.)

For all these reasons, as well as for a certain imposing breadth, it seems possible to think of the Primary-Minimal phenomenon as a "new academy"—if the term is properly pre-shrunk.

But even if we accept this for the sake of argument, it does not necessarily follow that it is a movement which produces academic work, in the well-known bad sense. Its characteristics of style and process do not inevitably result in a lack of imaginative variation, feeling, emotion or relevance, although all of this is sometimes deduced from its apparent taciturnity.

To accept this conclusion—a frequent enough accusation

—is to take a hard-boiled approach to the works themselves. Generalities about style, favorable or not, always apply with miserable imprecision to all the subtle reverberations of individual objects, and also overlook the vital question of differences of quality.

Although a widening-out process is going on, and although some of the adherents to the still-young Primary-Minimal movement are derivative, often "illustrating" ideas which were implicit in much earlier statements of the leaders, an academic congealment is not currently in process. On the contrary, a good deal of the work in this area which is obviously of doubtful quality is involved in a gradual, tentative elaboration of an esthetic position, and is interesting at least in this respect.

Intentionally destructive comparisons, which are frequently set up to ridicule the superficial similarities among many works, can also be revealing. It is essential to read not only the forms but especially the artists' differences of intent. Differences, disguised by blatant resemblances, exist where one does not expect to see them. Certain specifics—material, surface, proportion, scale, arrangement of multiple pieces— take on significance, from which can emanate the same almost unformulable variations that exist in many phases of past art whose extra-visual meaning is dead to us anyhow.

It should be accepted, in any case, before we even try to

evaluate the seemingly impersonal Primary-Minimal work, that there is such a thing as a style of the mind as well as of the hand.

This art is not academic—not repetitious, not even boring (although upon occasion this has been claimed for it as a "new" virtue). Deprived of so much, one is forced to see qualities which were given only peripheral value in earlier works. One of the inevitable consequences of a difficult shift in style is that it refines and intensifies the perceptions of the viewer. The drastic concentration becomes an attraction, only slightly perverse, very much in line with a current taste for ambiguity of value.

At the other pole from purist formalism is the fact that, as an outgrowth not only of Abstract-Expressionism but of the art of the early '60s, it has many impure elements which relate it to Pop—the quality of modern life is evoked by its industrial materials—deadpan, vulgar, brute, blunt or sleek— and by its abstract but incisive allusions to the commoner "invisible" parts of the urban and industrial landscape.

That it is sober and formal is not an inevitable sign of academism: subjugation of feeling can be a positive expression. Art has never been mere self-expression, but is involved in solutions to problems—form, meaning, or in between. The problem here is not only one of form, but also one of reference to human and inhuman scale, to the modern environment, to an architectural presence, to a threatening usurpation of the viewer's space, to an acceptance of the machine (that Bauhaus ideal which finally has taken root).

There are, of course, limitations, as with any deliberately extreme course of action. Having so reduced its preconditions, Minimal art nearly shuts off one of the principal directions in which it can evolve—toward refinement, intensification, a stripping down to essentials. Although limited possibilities are a characteristic of today's art, these artists operate in an area of risk where they can say everything or nothing, be profound or empty. In trying to avoid visual ambiguity, they may arrive at a moral and practical ambiguity. Worst of all, perhaps, is a tendency towards an isolationist, exclusivist assumption that art *has* to be a certain way.

But despite qualifying factors, and despite some curious and beguiling resemblances to academies of the past, this is not an academic movement. Above all it is not academic because it is personal and bizarre. Distillation to such a degree is inevitably odd. The work has exaggeration, tension, absurdity; its intellectual perversity, its negative content coexisting with a formal positive side, make it very pertinent to the present. Its position in today's wide spectrum, which is much more open than it was a decade ago, is not even as dominant as it seems. It is simply a powerful, productive, heterogeneous movement, with an extraordinary internal propulsion.

Stripped of their intellectual context, the works themselves are, like all valid art, the products of personal temperaments and individual sensibilities. However seductive generalities are, even to the artists, they have to be considered as subsidiaries, not inevitable adjuncts—the work stands alone, in the last analysis, as part of a visual continuity.

A footnote to the discussion of academies and the current scene: as the past keeps returning to revitalize the present in unexpected ways, some of the most despised characteristics of past academic art—its emphasis on meticulous execution and its elaborately staged, artificial figure compositions—are now beginning to interest some contemporary artists. Extremely relevant are the disjunctively combined, meticulously drawn, idealized fragments of bodies by Paul Waldman. Alfred Leslie is involved with heroic history painting. The "academic" as a subject (as differentiated from photo-derived figure painting) made a return in pre-Pop and Pop—Larry Rivers' *Washington Crossing the Delaware*, his re-working of David and Ingres portraits, his studies of parts of the body; Wesselmann's academic reclining nude (via Matisse); Martial Raysse's use of an Ingres odalisque; etc. Artists, being exceptionally receptive and open even to currently "unacceptable" sources, have continued to understand the value of past academies, and even of the academic. With the help of the avant-garde, the whole concept may regain a new currency.

Index

Page numbers in italics indicate colorplates

Advertisements

Pietro Antonio Martini: *The Salon of 1787 at the Louvre*, engraving.
At the lower left center hangs J. L. David's famous *Death of Socrates*.

*Serving Galleries, Collectors,
Artists, Interior Designers,
Dealers and Museums
Internationally—*

**Manufacturers of hand carved
period reproductions and
contemporary frames.**

**We have an outstanding
selection of polished aluminum
and brass frames.**

the Frameguild inc.

503 East 72nd Street, New York, N. Y. REgent 7-3572

Morris Broderson   Picador with Horse   1967

THE DOWNTOWN GALLERY 465 PARK AVENUE NEW YORK
ANKRUM GALLERY 657 NORTH LA CIENEGA BOULEVARD LOS ANGELES

New AND *Exciting*

ARTBOOKS FROM ABRAMS

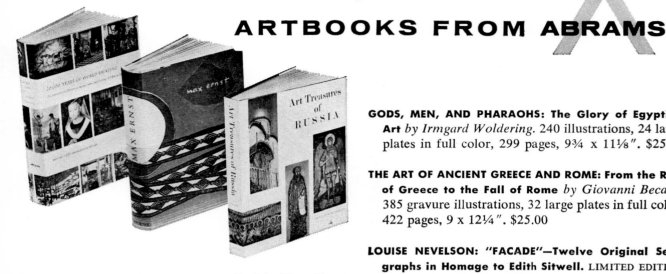

20,000 YEARS OF WORLD PAINTING *edited by Hans L. C. Jaffé.* 1,000 full color plates, 452 pages. $25.00

ART TREASURES OF RUSSIA *by M. W. Alpatov.* 104 tipped plates in full color, 180 pages. $25.00

PAUL KLEE *by Will Grohmann.* 138 illustrations, 48 large plates in full color, 160 pages, 9¾ x 12". $15.00

INGRES *by Robert Rosenblum.* 190 illustrations, 48 large plates in full color, 160 pages, 9¾ x 13". $20.00

MAX ERNST *by John Russell.* 475 illustrations, 49 large plates in full color, 354 pages, 8¼ x 11¾". $25.00

PICASSO: WOMEN *by Hélène Parmelin.* 160 hand-tipped plates in full color, 200 pages. $22.95

PEGGY GUGGENHEIM COLLECTION OF MODERN ART *by Nicolas Calas and Elena Calas.* 132 illustrations, 46 plates in full color, 320 pages. $25.00

GREEK ART AND ARCHITECTURE *by John Boardman, José Dörig, Werner Fuchs, and Max Hirmer.* 336 illustrations, 52 large plates in full color, plus 215 drawings and diagrams, 600 pages. $25.00.

TREASURES OF PREHISTORIC ART *by André Leroi-Gourhan.* 739 photographs, 121 large plates in full color, 187 drawings and diagrams, and 56 maps and charts, 500 pages, 9½ x 12⅛". $40.00

RODIN *by Bernard Champigneulle.* 116 illustrations, 16 plates in full color, 250 pages, 5⅞ x 8¼". $7.50

GODS, MEN, AND PHARAOHS: The Glory of Egyptian Art *by Irmgard Woldering.* 240 illustrations, 24 large plates in full color, 299 pages, 9¾ x 11⅛". $25.00

THE ART OF ANCIENT GREECE AND ROME: From the Rise of Greece to the Fall of Rome *by Giovanni Becatti.* 385 gravure illustrations, 32 large plates in full color, 422 pages, 9 x 12¼". $25.00

LOUISE NEVELSON: "FACADE"—Twelve Original Serigraphs in Homage to Edith Sitwell. LIMITED EDITION OF 125 COPIES. 12 originals, signed and numbered, 17 x 23", in black vinyl-covered box. $1,000

BRUEGEL AND LUCAS VAN LEYDEN: Complete Engravings, Etchings, and Woodcuts *by Jacques Lavalleye.* 491 black-and-white illustrations. $18.50

GREAT PRINTS AND PRINTMAKERS *by Herman J. Wechsler.* 137 illustrations, 16 hand-tipped plates in full color, 244 pages, 9¾ x 13". $25.00

GIACOMETTI: A SKETCHBOOK OF INTERPRETIVE DRAWINGS *by L. Carluccio.* 144 gravure illustrations in black-and-white, 328 pages, 8⅜ x 9½". $12.50

EARLY MEDIEVAL ART IN SPAIN *by Pedro de Palol, photographs by Max Hirmer.* 467 illustrations, 54 large plates in full color, plus 157 plans and maps, 534 pages, 9¼ x 12". $30.00

PORTRAITS AND PERSONALITIES: An Introduction to the World's Great Art *by Luise C. Kainz and Olive L. Riley.* 74 illustrations, 58 large plates in full color, 136 pages, 7⅝ x 10¾". $7.50

JAPANESE TEMPLES: Sculpture, Paintings, Gardens, and Architecture *by J. Edward Kidder, Jr.* 332 gravure illustrations, 14 large plates in full color, plus 24 diagrams and maps, 554 pages, 10 x 13½". $30.00

EXPRESSIONIST WATERCOLORS 1905—1920 *by Werner Hofmann.* 48 illustrations, 16 large matted facsimile reproductions in full color, 2 extra mats, 104 pages, 12 x 13". $20.00

WRITE FOR FREE CATALOGUE

HARRY N. ABRAMS, INC., 6 West 57th Street, New York 10019

A SUBSIDIARY OF THE TIMES MIRROR COMPANY

Marlborough
NEW YORK · LONDON · ROME

Marlborough-Gerson Gallery Inc.
41 East 57th Street
New York 10022
Agents for:
Mordecai Ardon
Naum Gabo
Juan Genoves
Adolph Gottlieb
Philip Guston
Lee Krasner
R B Kitaj
Jacques Lipchitz
Seymour Lipton
Conrad Marca-Relli
Robert Motherwell
Beverly Pepper
Larry Rivers
James Rosati
Mark Rothko
Julius Schmidt
Jesus Raphael Soto
James Wines
Fritz Wotruba
The Estate of William Baziotes

The Estate of Franz Kline
The Estate of David Smith
The Estate of Jackson Pollock

Marlborough Fine Art Ltd
39 Old Bond Street   London W1
Agents for:
Kenneth Armitage
Frank Auerbach
Francis Bacon
Lynn Chadwick
Günter Haese
Barbara Hepworth
Oskar Kokoschka
Richard Lin
Lucebert
Meier-Denninghoff
Henry Moore
Ben Nicholson
Sidney Nolan
Victor Pasmore
Roland Piché
John Piper

Paul Rebeyrolle
Ceri Richards
Graham Sutherland
Joe Tilson
Keith Vaughan
Brett Whiteley
The Estate of Willi Baumeister
The Estate of David Bomberg
The Estate of Kurt Schwitters

Marlborough Galleria d'Arte
via Gregoriana 5 · Rome
Agents for:
Pietro Consagra
Piero Dorazio
Lucio Fontana
Gastone Novelli
Achille Perilli
Arnaldo Pomodoro
Gio Pomodoro
Toti Scialoia
Emilio Vedova
The Estate of Spazzapan

159

St. Crispin's Day, October 25th, marks a significant anniversary in the development of one of America's most unusual artisan enterprises. Reviving a tradition which ended with the seventeenth century, St. Crispin now combines the classic functions of the publisher, printer, binder and bookseller in one establishment dedicated to the perfection of the book in all of its aspects.

The St. Crispin Bindery devotes itself to hand bindings in fine leather with the meticulous attention to detail and design that characterizes true craftsmanship. Significant contemporary titles are available from our shelves or books of your own choice can be bound to your specifications. The St. Crispin Workshop brings to cloth bindings a new emphasis on quality and style. Periodicals, catalogs, and other reference works are bound with the same care given to the more luxurious product of our leather Bindery.

The St. Crispin Press has been established to publish fine contemporary limited editions, and to do private edition printing of distinction and elegance. The work of the Press is done entirely by hand from hand-set type on hand-made rag paper. Among its first titles for fall, three are noteworthy in the contemporary art world: "Points of Departure", by George Reavey, with an original signed engraving by S. W. Hayter; "Arts and Ends", critical and personal essays by Julien Levy, with previously unpublished drawings by Arshile Gorky, Tchelitchew and Leonor Fini; and "Homage to Robert W. Service", the first assembly of prints by CPLY, signalling a new approach to processes in printmaking.

The St. Crispin Studio offers professional instruction in fine binding by one of today's most creative and talented bookbinders. Personal attention and extensive shop facilities and materials are available for all levels of competence. Guest lecturers of authority in binding and related fields, and invitation exhibitions of the work of outstanding binders, will also be a part of the program of the Studio as the focus of bookbinding interest in America.

888 MADISON AVENUE NEW YORK 10021 ✦ UN 1-9090

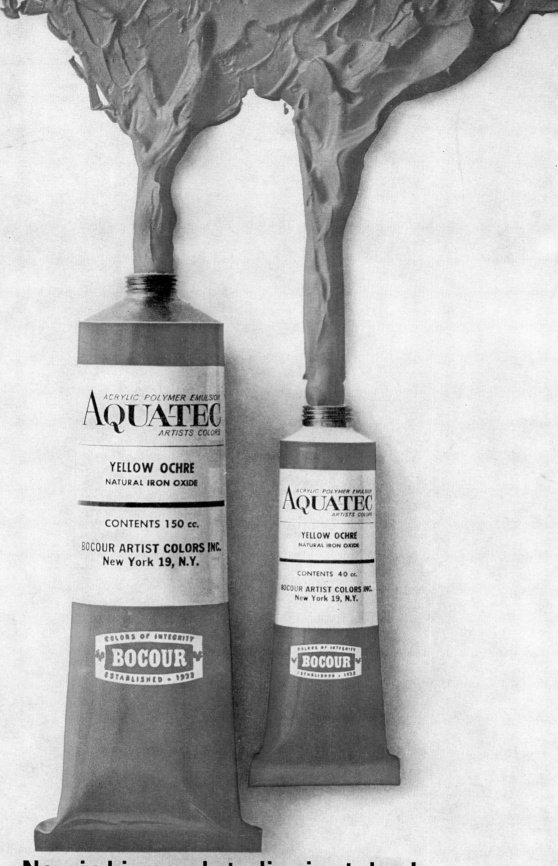

Now in king and studio size tubes!

Aquatec is a water-based artist color, made with 100% acrylic polymer emulsion. It is the finest, most versatile, color-rich medium an artist can use. Developed to provide free and expressive new techniques from thin wash to heavy impasto, without fear of darkening or cracking. It comes to you from Bocour, America's originator of acrylic resins for artist use. Take advantage of our special introductory tube offer: a working palette of 11 studio-size colors, plus Aquatec Jel and a king-size tube of Titanium White, only $6.95.* Check or money-order ...no COD's. For full information on how to use Aquatec, write Bocour Artist Colors, Inc., 552 W. 52nd St., N.Y. 10019.

AQUATEC is available at all leading art supply stores everywhere.

*N.Y.C. RESIDENTS ADD 5% SALES TAX.

Oil on Cardboard   25 x 20 Inches

"LA FIANCEE"

MARC CHAGALL

Signed: Lower Right: Marc Chagall

Reproduced: **Marc Chagall** *by Franz Meyer, 1961, no. 542*

HIRSCHL & ADLER *Galleries inc.*

21 E. 67th St · NY 21 · LE 5-8810

FRANK CARO

Porcelain
altar incense burner,
K'ang Hsi period
(1662-1722)
Height 6½ inches.

41 EAST 57TH STREET
NEW YORK CITY
AREA CODE (212) PL. 3-2166

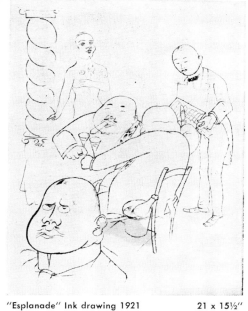

M. KNOEDLER & CO., INC.

14 East 57th Street, New York, N.Y. 10022

DALI · DE KOONING · NAY
VIEIRA DA SILVA · SOULAGES
BRAM VAN VELDE · WYETH

CALLERY · HAJDU · MOORE
CHADWICK · LARDERA · ROSENTHAL

October 10 - November 4, 1967

DUCHAMP-VILLON

November 14 - December 2, 1967

DE KOONING

December 5 - 29, 1967

SPACE AND DREAM

New York Telephone: (212) PLAZA 3-9742
CABLE ADDRESSES "KNOEDLER" NEW YORK, PARIS, LONDON

PARIS 85bis FAUBOURG ST. HONORÉ
LONDON, 34 ST. JAMES'S STREET

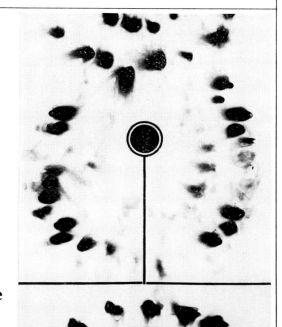

Do you know about THE AMERICAN FEDERATION OF ARTS?

10 THINGS AFA DOES:

1 subsidizes and circulates *exhibitions* of painting, sculpture and architecture for small museums, colleges and art centers. Last year it had more than 450 showings of 90 different exhibitions throughout the United States   **2** publishes *books* and *catalogs* of lasting importance, not only catalogs of exhibitions **3** produces a *curriculum of visual education for* elementary and secondary schools   **4** promotes international goodwill through the *exchange of exhibitions* with Europe and the Far East   **5** plans *educational tours* to little known culture areas throughout the world   **6** arranges through an Anonymous Donor Program for the purchase of works of art for museums with limited funds   **7** conducts an *art critics Workshop*   **8** invites contributions from industry for the encouragement of painting, sculpture and the decorative arts   **9** organizes and circulates a program of *films on art*   **10** actively supports legislation which is beneficial to the art world

10 REASONS FOR JOINING AFA

$18 ANNUAL MEMBERSHIP ENTITLES YOU TO:

1 Free annual subscription to *Art News* or *Art in America* or *Arts* or *Art International*
2 25 percent discount on most art books
3 Complimentary annual subscription to *The Art Gallery*
4 Complimentary annual subscription to *Chicago Midwest Art* to all members in Midwestern states
5 Special discounts on 26 magazines related to the arts
6 20 percent discount on membership in International Graphic Arts Society
7 Special discounts on AFA Reference Books: *The American Art Directory* and *Who's Who in American Art*
8 Special rates for subscriptions to *Art News*, *Art in America*, *Arts* and *Art International*
9 Invitation to Openings of AFA Exhibitions and announcements of special art events
10 Invitation to AFA Meetings and Symposia

Detach coupon and mail now

MEMBERS WHO CONTRIBUTE $35 or more in Annual Dues receive, in addition to all other benefits, catalogs of oustanding exhibitions distributed periodically, selections from AFA Special Publication Series, and a ticket admitting TWO to a Very Special Event that is held each fall in New York City.

- ☐ $ 18 Active
- ☐ $ 35 Contributing
- ☐ $ 65 Supporting
- ☐ $100 Sustaining
- ☐ $250 Sponsor
- ☐ $500 Patron

CHECK ONE:
- ☐ Art News
- ☐ Art in America
- ☐ Arts
- ☐ Art International

MEMBERS WHO CONTRIBUTE $65 or more in Annual Dues, in addition to all other benefits, receive complimentary subscriptions to TWO of the four art magazines, a complimentary copy of Art News Annual, *all* volumes issued in the AFA Special Publication Series, and on request may be enrolled as members of the International Graphic Arts Society.

NAME ....

ADDRESS ....

CITY .... **STATE** .... **ZIP** .... ana

THE AMERICAN FEDERATION OF ARTS, 41 E. 65th St., New York, N. Y. 10021

The American Federation of Arts was founded in 1909. Incorporated in 1916 as a non-profit educational organization.

SUPPORT THIS NATIONAL ART ORGANIZATION THROUGH MEMBERSHIP

Put together
beautifully. Nice
contrast in texture.
Fouke-dyed Black
Alaska fur seal,
the limited edition fur.
And shiny young vinyl.
By that well-known
architect,

GEORGES
Kaplan
730 FIFTH AVENUE, N.Y.

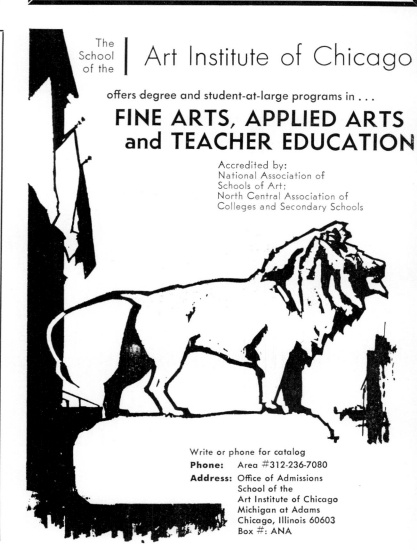

CLEVELAND INSTITUTE OF ART

PROFESSIONAL TRAINING

Painting Sculpture
Printmaking
Industrial Design
Graphic Design
Photography
Ceramics
Weaving Textiles
Silversmithing
Enameling
Teacher Training

DEGREES-SCHOLARSHIPS
CATALOG ON REQUEST
Write: Director of Admissions,
11141 East Boulevard,
Cleveland, Ohio 44106

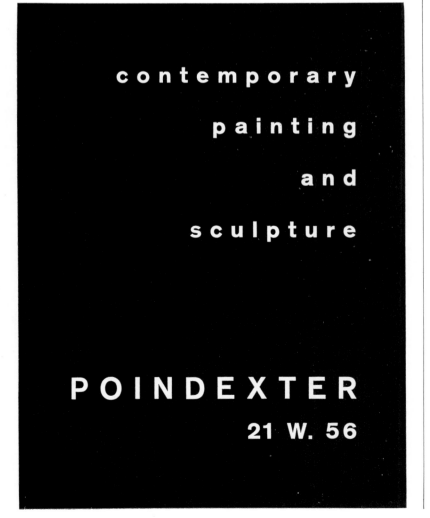

What do you think is the most important ability for an artist?

To me, drawing is the most important. Unless you know how to draw, you won't know the security of being able to express yourself clearly and fluently as an artist. If you are able to draw, you can devote yourself to saying what you think and feel. The more you know about drawing, the more productively creative you can be. You are no longer concerned with "how" to draw, but rather "what" to draw.

How were you trained, Mr. Giusti? As a designer or painter?

Actually, I was trained as an architect. I went to the Academy of Brera, in Milan, where I learned all the rudiments of art—perspective, drawing, painting. It was very strict formal training. We did everything—copying of casts, studying of anatomy. It was thorough training, training from the ground up.

What would you say, Mr. Giusti, is the ideal curriculum for someone who wants to study design?

Well, he should study the fundamental theory of design—division of space, balance, relationship between elements, color, technique, drawing. I think academic drawing is very important.

Do you advocate specialization to beginners?

No. I think to be versatile is the best way—to be able to do packages, illustrations, book jackets. I tried a little bit of everything before I found that whatever I'm doing at the moment is what I like to do best.

What advice would you give to a young person embarking on a career in design?

I would advise him to get the most thorough training available. Discipline is the most important ingredient. I think it is good

for a student who wants to enter the design field to try several branches instead of settling into one. He might try an advertising agency for a year, then go to work for a publishing house and see how this kind of design is done. He could work as an interior designer or try package design. But, definitely, he should try several branches of design work.

•   •   •

George Giusti is hailed as one of America's foremost designers and art directors. He has been honored with more than one hundred important awards in the graphic-arts field, including the coveted Golden T-Square of the National Society of Art Directors. Portfolios of his work have appeared in many international art magazines.

In January, 1959, Giusti joined the Guiding Faculty of the Famous Artists School of Westport, Connecticut. To make sure the students of this world-famous home-study art school are prepared to meet the challenge of the future, Giusti created an outstanding and extensive course on contemporary design and layout. This course is included in the School's highly successful course in Commercial Art, Illustration and Design.

If you are an ambitious artist, anxious to get ahead, you may want to consider taking the course created by Giusti, Rockwell, Fuchs, Peak—and many more of America's most famous artists. You can study at home in your spare time.

For further information, at no cost or obligation to you, simply mail the coupon below.

The Famous Artists School is directed by:

Norman Rockwell	Tom Allen	Julian Levi
Al Parker	Lorraine Fox	Joseph Hirsch
Ben Stahl	Franklin McMahon	
Stevan Dohanos	———	Milton Caniff
Jon Whitcomb	Ben Shahn	Al Capp
Peter Helck	Doris Lee	Dick Cavalli
Austin Briggs	Dong Kingman	Whitney Darrow Jr.
Harold Von Schmidt	Arnold Blanch	Rube Goldberg
George Giusti	Adolf Dehn	Harry Haenigsen
Fred Ludekens	Fletcher Martin	Willard Mullin
Bernard Fuchs	Will Barnet	Virgil Partch
Bob Peak	Syd Solomon	Barney Tobey

An encyclopedic view of the nature of vision in contemporary culture

VISION+VALUE
Edited by GYORGY KEPES

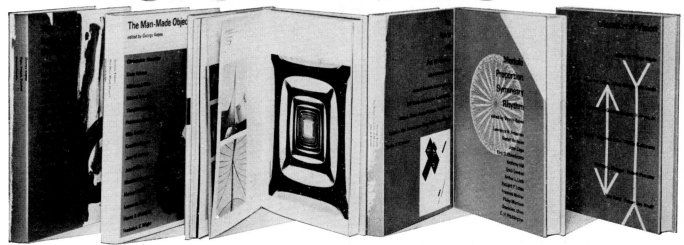

YOURS FOR ONLY $2.95 A VOLUME
—A SAVINGS OF MORE THAN 75% OFF RETAIL ($12.50 PER VOLUME)—WITH MEMBERSHIP IN THE SEVEN ARTS BOOK SOCIETY

"We are alienated from our environment, each other and ourselves. Specialization and a logarithmic rate of change are reducing our experience to a chaos of discreet events. We live in an era of man-made formlessness and turmoil unparalleled in our history or in nature.

"These are the dire conditions that Gyorgy Kepes, painter, designer, author and professor of visual design at Massachusetts Institute of Technology, has the temerity to challenge with his *Vision + Value* series. He sets out to prove that the contemporary alienations are not necessary, that they are only the results of an outdated point of view of ourselves and our environment. For this purpose he has collected in six volumes some hundred superbly illustrated essays by 84 distinguished natural and social scientists, architects, artists and critics from a dozen countries."—Roger Jellenek, *New York Times Book Review*

"Great significance"

"The *Vision + Value* series aims at the reintegration of our contemporary scientific, social and artistic environment. The educational method involved is essentially visual, the 'design,' whether revealed by science, constructed by the intellect or created by the imagination, being the connecting link between the various disciplines.... What needs to be emphasized, and what is emphasized by Professor Kepes and his fellow contributors, is the unitary nature of the process. It is not a question of bringing art and science together in some kind of armistice, but rather a single integrated process of visual education, of 'interseeing' of the same phenomena. This is an educational enterprise of great significance, and those who ignore it will be missing one of the most exciting and progressive developments in the whole field of education."—Sir Herbert Read

"The work brought to focus in this series is highly significant, and it stands high above any similar effort, by reason of its scale, its scope, and its depth."—Lewis Mumford

Each volume in the *Vision + Value* series is devoted to a broad basic theme which, because of its common or related meaning to different professional concepts, provides fruitful ground for confronting, combining and comparing knowledge from diverse disciplines. Scientists will find here a key to artistic values, and artists the vision of the scientist's world. For architects and city planners who structure our contemporary world, for scholars, educators and students, here is the pulse of ideas in the making, the scope of today's problems. For the general reader, these books provide an invaluable guide to the cultural landscape. Each volume, whose contents were written expressly for this series, is approximately 256 pages, measures $8^7/_8$" x $10^7/_8$", and contains 150 extraordinary illustrations.

CONTRIBUTORS

The Education of Vision: Rudolf Arnheim • Mirko Basaldella • Julian Beinart • Will Burtin • Anton Ehrenzweig • William J. J. Gordon • Bartlett H. Hayes, Jr. • Gerald Holton • Johannes Itten • Tomás Maldonado • Wolfgang Metzger • Robert Preusser • Paul Rand • Robert Jay Wolff

The Nature and Art of Motion: James S. Ackerman • Donald Appleyard • Gillo Dorfles • Karl Gerstner • Robert Gessner • James J. Gibson • Stanley W. Hayter • Gerald Holton • Katharine Kuh • Hans Richter • George Rickey • Hans Wallach • Gordon B. Washburn

Structure in Art and in Science: Max Bill • Jacob Bronowski • R. Buckminster Fuller • Richard Held • H. L. C. Jaffé • Richard Lippold • F. Maki & M. Ohtaka • Pier Luigi Nervi • I. A. Richards • Eduard F. Sekler • Cyril Stanley Smith • Alison & Peter Smithson • Margit Staber • Lancelot L. Whyte

The Man-Made Object: Christopher Alexander • Dore Ashton • Michael J. Blee • Marcel Breuer • Theodore M. Brown • Françoise Choay • Gillo Dorfles • Kazuhiko Egawa • Joan M. Erikson • Jean Hélion • Marshall McLuhan • Herbert Read • L. Ricci • Henry S. Stone, Jr. • F. S. Wight

Module, Proportion, Symmetry, Rhythm: Lawrence B. Anderson • R. Arnheim • John Cage • Ezra D. Ehrenkrantz • Anthony Hill • E. Lendvai • Arthur L. Loeb • R. P. Lohse • François Molnar • Philip Morrison • Stanislaw Ulam • C. H. Waddington

Sign, Image, Symbol: Rudolf Arnheim • Saul Bass • Ludwig von Bertalanffy • John E. Burchard • Edmund Carpenter • Henry Dreyfuss • Heinz Von Foerster • Lawrence K. Frank • James J. Gibson • S. Giedion • J. P. Hodin • Abraham H. Maslow • P. A. Michelis • Rudolf Modley • C. Morris & F. Sciadini • Robert Osborn • Ad Reinhardt • Paul Riesman • Ernesto N. Rogers • W. Schmalenbach

If you appreciate fine books on the arts – books, such as the internationally acclaimed *Vision + Value* series, membership in the Seven Arts Book Society will enable you to obtain these books conveniently and economically.

From the many books on painting, sculpture, architecture, design, city-planning and the other arts, Seven Arts selections are among the most important and authoritative of each season. As a member you will have the opportunity to obtain these books at substantial savings—lavishly illustrated, handsomely bound volumes, each an elegant and essential addition to your personal art library. You will receive free each month the illustrated *Seven Arts News* which reviews the many fine books available to members.

We invite you to enroll in this unique Society. As a special introductory offer, you may choose any of the volumes of the *Vision + Value* series at only $2.95 per volume (retail $12.50)—or, if you wish, all 6 volumes at only $15.95—a savings of more than 75% off retail prices.

175

Vice-President in charge of good taste:

If a man wants
to put up a
building
in the shape of an
elephant,
there are just two
restraints that can
prevent such a
monstrosity:
(1) A strong building code,
(2) An adviser with a sense
of good taste.
When man uproots nature,
taking away trees, flowers,
rocks and beauty,
he has an obligation to do
something beautiful in return.
Monotonous look-alike housing
developments are not enough.
Cigar-box buildings are not enough.
Public housing projects, lined up like
file drawers are not enough.
Tasteless, hungry developers
will build anything as long
as you'll buy it.
Governments, business firms,
clubs and families should appoint
a Vice-President in charge of
good taste.
Then someday "American Beauty"
will stand for
An American Rose,
An American Woman,
An American Building.

This
message
is from...

Newsweek